THE COMPLETE GUIDE TO
SINGLE-ENGINE
BEECHCRAFTS
-2nd Edition

THE COMPLETE GUIDE TO
SINGLE-ENGINE
BEECHCRAFTS
-2nd Edition

BY JOE CHRISTY

MODERN AVIATION SERIES

TAB BOOKS

BLUE RIDGE SUMMIT, PA. 17214

FIRST EDITION

FIRST PRINTING—MAY 1979

Copyright © 1979 by TAB BOOKS

Printed in the United States of America

Library of Congress Cataloging in Publication Data

Christy, Joe.
  The complete guide to single-engine Beechcrafts.

  First ed. published in 1970 under title: The single-engine Beechcrafts.
  Includes index.
  1. Beechcraft (Airplanes) I. Title.
TL686.B36C47 1979   629.133′343   79-12600
ISBN 0-8306-9791-8
ISBN 0-8306-2258-6 pbk.

Contents

Olive Ann Beech, chief executive officer of Beech Aircraft Corporation.

1. The Beginning

AIRPLANES HAVE ALWAYS been built mostly by hand. This fact once led the late Walter H. Beech to remark, "In no other manufacturing business is the human element more vital than in the building of an airplane."

Proper and continuing recognition of this truth seems to be a chief reason for Beech's success. From the beginning, Walter Beech appears to have hired not workers but disciples, always choosing people with an unusual pride in their work. Even today, down on the production lines at the Beech main plant, it's easy to get the impression that these people are building airplanes because they'd rather do it than anything else in the world—and that the only reason they take pay for it is because their wives (or maybe the union) insists upon it.

Such *esprit de corps* among 12,000 Beechcrafters is reflected in the fact that (at this writing) there's never been a strike at Beech, and more than one-third of all personnel have over ten years' service with the company. It is therefore not surprising that when a recent visitor to the Wichita plant voiced the opinion that the elaborate airframe inspection system must be costly, a foreman was quick to reply: "Mister, we'll let somebody else build the cheapest planes possible—we'd rather build the best!" Walter Beech would have liked that.

Walter was born January 30, 1891, in Pulaski, Tennessee. At the age of fourteen he built a crude glider which he crashed on its maiden flight (this was just two years after the Wright brothers flew at Kitty Hawk). He finally soloed a Curtiss pusher biplane in 1914. After serving as a pilot in World War I, Walter turned to barnstorming, employed by Pete Hill and Erret Williams at Arkansas City, Kansas.

In 1921, he joined the E. M. Laird Airplane Company in Wichita as a test pilot and salesman of the Laird Swallow. The Swallow,

Walter H. Beech, founder of Beech Aircraft Corporation.

an OX-5-powered biplane, was the product of Matty Laird (later famous for his commercial and racing planes built in Chicago), and was sold to flying schools, barnstormers, and a few businessmen who were ahead of the times.

By 1924 Laird had left the company and Walter had moved up to general manager under owner Jake Moellendick. Then Walter quit to form his own company after a disagreement over construction methods and materials. Moellendick insisted that the Swallow fuselage continue to be made of wood, while Walter was convinced that steel tubing would be stronger and better.

Travel Air Is Born. Thus, in the fall of 1924, the Travel Air Company came into existence. In addition to Walter and an attractive young woman named Olive Ann Mellor, who served as secretary and office manager, the new company was made up of Lloyd Stearman, Clyde Cessna, and a half-dozen skilled workers. The "factory" was a 30-foot-square building behind the Broadview Hotel in Wichita.

The first Travel Air was a three-place open-cockpit biplane powered with the ubiquitous OX-5 engine. It was a handsome and sturdy craft with a steel tube fuselage and it proved a reliable performer. It was flown and praised by an unknown airmail pilot named Charles Lindbergh. Nineteen Travel Airs were built and sold by the end of 1925.

Travel Air E-4000 was powered with a Wright J6–5 engine of 165 hp. It cruised at 103 mph; had a top of 122 mph; landed at 46 mph; climb was 700 fpm, range 690 miles, ceiling 13,000 feet.

During the next four years the Travel Air Company became the world's largest producer of commercial airplanes. Meanwhile, both Cessna and Stearman left to form companies of their own. (There were no hard feelings involved in the separations. It was just that three giants in a single castle were too many.)

Following Walter's formula for rugged, carefully built aircraft, the business grew rapidly. By 1929 Travel Air had delivered 307 planes to buyers throughout the world, the company was occupying five buildings on East Central Avenue (site of the main Beech plant today), and it employed 650 men. An example of the confidence generated by Walter's policies is illustrated by the following wire recently found in Beech files:

```
Fort Worth, Texas              April 19, 1929

Walter Beech
Travel Air Company
Wichita, Kansas

Build me whatever you think I ought to
have.

              Regards,
              Tom Hardin, Texas Air Transport.
```

Of course, the Travel Airs were not as efficient as modern airplanes, but in those days of small sod airports, short landing and take-off runs were of greater importance than high cruising speeds. A cruise of 100 miles per hour was acceptable for a plane that could land at 40 or 45—and could get out of a 300-foot pea patch surrounded by "bob-wire."

A 1929 Travel Air sales brochure listed nine biplane models and three cabin monoplanes. Actually, this amounted to a single biplane design with a choice of nine different powerplants; two six-place high-wing monoplanes (actually the same plane with a choice of two engines), and a four-place high-wing cabin monoplane. According to the brochure, the biplane customer paid extra if he wanted any color except blue with orange wings. Other options included Oleo, or rubber shock-cord "chassis," Spanish leather or Fabrikoid upholstering, and inset or balanced ("elephant ear") ailerons.

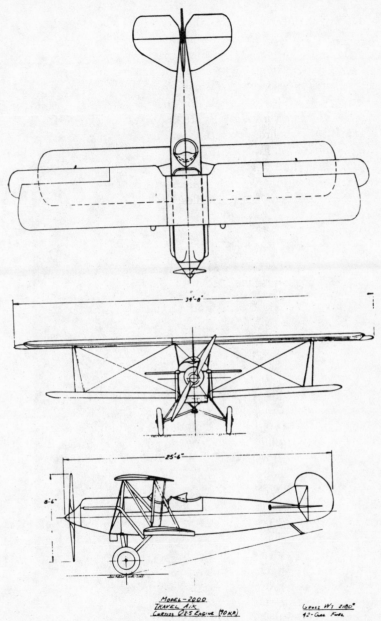

MODEL-2000
TRAVEL AIR
CURTISS OX-5 ENGINE (90 H.P.)

GROSS WT 2180#
42-GAL FUEL

Travel Air Model 2000, often called the "Wichita Fokker," was fitted with Curtiss OX-5 engine of 90 hp. It sold for $3,500. It had a top speed of 100 mph, landed at 42 mph, and had a normal cruising range of 400 miles. There were 1,166 built.

Travel Air 6000B was a 6-place craft intended for fledgling airlines and the first businessmen-pilots. Engine was Wright J6–9 of 300 hp; top speed 135 mph; cruise 110; landed at 60 mph, had useful load of 1,530 lbs. and gross weight of 4,320 lbs.

The Glamorous Mystery S. But the proudest Travel Air of all was the Model R, commonly called the "Mystery S." The Mystery S was a glamor gal, and she started a revolution in airplane design. Built in secrecy during the summer of 1929, and unveiled just in time to enter the National Air Races at Cleveland, this advanced design created a sensation.

Aerodynamically clean, with a thin low wing and speed fairings covering her wheels, the Mystery S looked fast. She was. She could get over 230 mph out of her souped-up Wright 300 engine.

The Mystery S could—and did—literally fly circles around the military biplane fighters of almost twice her horsepower. She performed this feat in the first Thompson Trophy Race when pilot Doug Davis turned in mid-course to re-circle a pylon he thought he had missed. He went on to win, and though his average speed was cut to 194.9 mph by his turn-around, the little Travel Air crossed the finish line far ahead of the second-place P3A Hawk entered by the Army Air Corps.

Later, a pair of Travel Air Mystery Ships flown by Frank Hawks and Jimmy Doolittle toured the country breaking records and collecting prize money.

The lesson offered by this Beech product was plain. Nearly all subsequent racing planes were of similar low-wing configuration—and the military fighters soon followed suit.

In the fall of 1929 the Travel Air Company was merged into what was then the huge Curtiss-Wright complex. Walter was expected to remain as a vice-president of the Curtiss-Wright Corporation and president of the Airplane Division; but the plush offices in New York City were too far removed from the production lines, drafting rooms, and sod airfields where the real action was. He resigned, and in 1932—near the low point of the worst depression the world had seen—he and Olive Ann, whom he had married in 1930, and a handful of optimistic associates organized Beech Aircraft Company.

The Classic Staggerwing. Less than a dozen employees were on the payroll when work began on Walter's newest product. This aircraft, a cabin biplane, was called Model 17. And it became a classic.

Today, it is usually referred to as the Staggerwing Beech, be-

Travel Air "Mystery Ship" (Model R) was an advanced design for 1929. It won the first Thompson Trophy race in Cleveland that year, and influenced subsequent racer and military fighter designs. Five were built and fitted with several different engines, though the fastest one (230 mph) had a Wright R-975 of 420 hp.

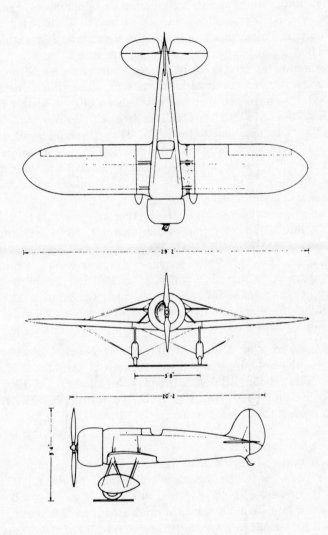

TRAVEL AIR COMPANY
Wichita, Kan.
MODEL R
1 PLACE
ENGINE: SPECIAL WRIGHT WHIRLWIND 300

cause its lower wings are placed ahead of its upper ones—negatively staggered. And it's possible that, as you read this, a Staggerwing Beech sits confidently out there on the flight line. It remained in production for sixteen years, and many are still flying.

The impressive record of the Staggerwing seems to be owed to two things: Walter's original formula—a rugged airframe, carefully built—plus performance that was years ahead of its contemporaries. The first one, NC499N, powered with a 420 hp Wright engine, cruised at 180 mph and topped 201. Those that followed (more than 700 were eventually built) were fitted with a number of different engines: from the 225 Jacobs to the 700 hp Wright Cyclone. This latter model, of which two were built, offered a cruising speed of 235 mph at 13,000 feet!

During the next few years, Beech Aircraft grew slowly, though steadily. But in the early thirties mere survival was considered an accomplishment. Then, in 1937, Walter produced another classic.

This one was the Model 18, a twin-engine, low-wing cabin monoplane. And no string of superlatives could describe its rugged quality better than the following single fact: On January 15, 1969, the Model 18 completed its 32nd year of continuous production! No other airplane in history has ever approached this record.[1]

Beech Goes to War. During World War II Beech built Staggerwings for the military, and military versions of the Model 18: the AT-7, AT-11, C-45, JRB and SNB; plus the all-wood AT-10 which had no civilian counterpart. Also developed was the XA-38 Grizzly, a twin-engine attack craft mounting a 75 mm cannon, which was faster than a P-51. The war ended, however, before the Grizzly was put into production.

Four months after V J Day, Beech rolled out the prototype of another pace-setter, the Beechcraft Bonanza, Model 35. Certificated in November, 1946, Bonanza deliveries began the following February. More than 500 advance orders, with cash deposits, were received for the Bonanza even before pictures of it were released. The faith revealed in Tom Hardin's telegram sixteen years previously was stronger than ever.

---

[1] Perhaps it is interesting to note that in 1937 three companies dominated the field of general aviation. These were Beech, Cessna, and Piper. Beech was making two planes—the Model 17 and the Model 18. Cessna had but one, the Airmaster. Piper was offering the Cub.

2. Beechcraft Model 17 Staggerwing

It has been more than twenty years since the last Staggerwing was built, but most aviation people agree that she's still a magnificent flying machine. Originally designed in 1932, the Model 17 Beechcraft will get up and go with the latest Model 35 Bonanza.

Altogether, 781 Staggerwings were built between 1932 and 1949. Of these, 427 were produced for the military between 1935 and 1944. Of the 353 civilian Staggerwings made, one, a D17W powered with a 600 hp Pratt & Whitney and flown by Jackie Cochran in the Bendix race, was never certificated by the CAA (now FAA), and went into Army service at beginning of World War II. Although there were only 352 Model 17's built for the civilian market, a substantial number of the military models found their way into civilian hands via the surplus market after the war to swell this figure.

The first Model 17 Staggerwing had fixed gear enclosed in streamlined pants. Nevertheless, this craft did over 200 mph with a 420 hp engine.

Actually, Beech didn't intend to build this plane after introduction of the new Bonanza in 1946, but some prewar Staggerwing owners insisted that the 165 hp odd-tailed Bonanza was no replacement for the last of the great biplanes. Walter Beech appreciated such devotion and produced on special order an additional sixteen civilian models (G17S) priced at $29,000.

In 1969, about 250 Staggerwings were still registered or in the process of being restored. Prices on the used plane market ranged between $7,000 and $10,000 when they could be found, although a really good one could run much higher. Many were simply not for sale, period.

A lot of hangar talk has been devoted to the Staggerwing's flying habits over the years, and since pilots generally—and veteran pilots in particular—are, for some perverse reason, given either to understatement or overstatement (probably depending upon whether they like you or not), they don't always tell it like it is when describing the Model 17's handling characteristics. One will tell you that it flies "just like a big Cub." Another will warn you to treat it with care and respect.

In truth, the Staggerwing is not a tricky airplane to fly. But you can bash one on landing roll-out if you don't hold her straight after losing rudder control. Early Staggerwings were the worst potential ground-loopers because of a one-foot-shorter fuselage. This is, of course, no problem for any reasonably competent pilot with tail-dragger experience.

In flight, the plane is very stable around its pitch axis and unstable laterally along its roll axis. It has no dihedral; put a wing down and it stays there. Controls are very solid all the way down to 100 mph. Below 90, the solid feel begins to go a little soggy, although the airplane is amazingly stall-resistant because the lower wing has incidence and the upper wing has not. Therefore the lower wing stalls first. So, you really have to work at it to stall this airplane, and even then the break is gentle. When the top wing finally stalls, the nose drops and you are flying again. The stall comes at about 60 mph, power off.

Best cruise in the D17S Model is achieved at 9,700 feet, where full throttle will produce 202-204 mph on about 25 gph fuel consumption. At a little less altitude, you can get an economy cruise of 100 mph IAS with about 9 gph. In between, 50% power will

Beechcraft G17S Staggerwing was post-WW II model. Sixteen were built, powered with P&W R-985 engines of 450 hp.

Model D17W was one of a kind; built in 1937 and flown principally as a racer by Aviatrix Jackie Cochran. Engine was an uprated Wasp of 600 hp.

give you a true air speed in excess of 170 mph on approximately seventeen gallons per hour of fuel expended.

Normal take-off (don't raise the tail too soon or you'll invite a groundloop) requires about 1,200 feet of runway to clear a 50-foot obstacle, and she lifts off at 65 mph within fifteen to seventeen seconds. Climb will exceed 1,000 fpm at about 110 IAS.

Original Construction Data Model D17S

Fuselage: Chrome molybdenum steel tubing structure with spruce and plywood fairings to shape contour to proper aerodynamic dimensions. All fairings jig-built as units and riveted to the fuselage, at many points only a few inches apart. Front of fuselage, back to and including the door, metal covered. Landing gear trusses heat treated; longerons and trusses Lionoil treated inside, pressure tested, and hermetically sealed.

Wings: Solid spruce spars and ribs, fabric covered. Rib spacing, 6½ inches. Duralumin leading edge and plywood-covered wing tips of low-loss design. Heat-treated chrome moly steel "I" struts between upper and lower wing panels. Alloy steel streamlined flying and landing wires are in duplicate, each of which will safely carry the maximum applied load.

Tail group: The fixed surfaces are of cantilever construction and no struts or bracing wires are used. Both solid and laminated spruce spars are used. Spruce ribs and plywood leading edges provide necessary aerodynamic form. Control surfaces are built of chrome moly steel tubing, fabric covered. Both elevator and rudder are provided with trim tabs, controllable from either front seat of the cabin. The leading edges are covered with two thicknesses of fabric, as are the bottom surfaces of the horizontal stabilizer and elevator.

Ailerons: Full-length aerodynamically and statically balanced ailerons are attached to the upper wings. Ball bearings are used throughout.

Flaps: Full-length aerodynamically balanced trailing edge flaps are attached to lower wings. These flaps are mechanically interconnected and are driven by an electric motor controlled by a three-way switch located on the instrument panel. They may be stopped or reversed at any point within their travel. Limit switches automatically stop the motor at the full-up and full-down positions. The flap location eliminates any effect upon control surfaces; and landing trim of the airplane is improved by depressing the flaps.

Propeller: Hamilton standard controllable pitch propeller with manual control located on the instrument panel.

Staggerwing Model E17B was built in May, 1937, and powered with a Jacobs L-5 engine of 285 hp.

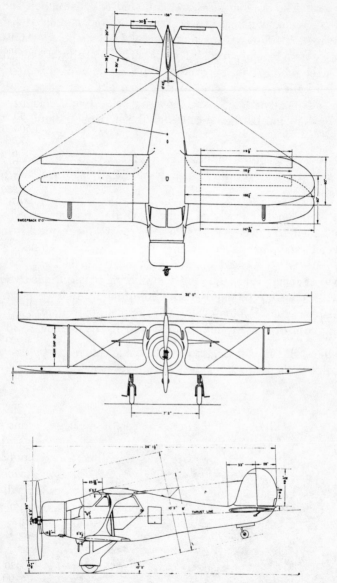

Staggerwing D17S, built for the military, was rigged with five degrees incidence in both wings. Most other Stagger-Wings had incidence in bottom wing only.

MODEL D17S PERFORMANCE AND SPECIFICATIONS

Engine: Pratt & Whitney nine cylinder, SB Wasp Junior rated at 400 hp at 2,200 rpm at 5,000 feet; cruise rating, 300 hp at 2,000 rpm at 9,600 feet; power available for take-off, 450 hp at 2,300 rpm at 36.5 inches manifold pressure. Compression ratio, 6:1; blower ratio, 10:1; fuel, 80/87 octane. Generator, 12–14 volts.

Top speed .... 212 mph
Cruising speed, 9,700 ft .... 202 mph
Landing speed, sea level, std. atmosphere .... 50 mph
Climb rate, initial .... 1,500 fpm
Service ceiling .... 25,000 ft
Take-off run, sea level, std. atmosphere .... 610 ft
Take-off run over 50-ft obstacle .... 1,200 ft
Landing run, sea level, std. atmosphere .... 750 ft
Landing run to clear 50-ft obstacle .... 1,250 ft
Cruising range with 45-minute reserve .... 670 mi

SPECIFICATIONS, MODEL D17S

Wing span .... 32 ft
Length .... 26 ft, 10.7 in
Height .... 8 ft
Wing area .... 296.5 sq ft
Power loading .... 10.5 lbs/hp
Wing loading .... 14.7 lbs/sq ft
Gross weight .... 4,200 lbs
Empty weight .... 2,540 lbs
Useful load .... 1,660 lbs
Baggage .... 125 lbs.
Fuel capacity .... 100 gal
Oil capacity .... 6½ gal
Seating capacity .... 4 or 5 passengers

A total of 276 Model D-17S Staggerwings were built, 223 of these for the military (many later returned to civil use), thus the D17S was by far the most numerous of the Staggerwings. The G17S, built after World War II, was also fitted with the P&W R-985 engine of 450 hp and had similar performance. As previously mentioned, only sixteen of the postwar G17S's were produced.

Total Staggerwing production table below was taken from the Wichita *Eagle* and compiled by John Zimmerman.

Model	Year	Production	Engine	
17R	1932-1933	2	Wright	420 hp
A17F	1934-1935	2	Wright	700 hp
B17L	1934-1936	46	Jacobs	225 hp
B17E	1935-1936	5	Wright	285 hp
B17R[1]	1935-1936	15 (3)[2]	Wright	420 hp

Model	Year	Production	Engine		
C17L[1]	1936-1937	5 (3)	Jacobs	225	hp
C17R[1]	1936-1937	16 (5)	Wright	420	hp
C17B[1]	1936-1937	40 (10)	Jacobs	285	hp
C17E	1936	1	Wright	285	hp
D17S[1]	1937-1944	53 (223)	P & W	450	hp
D17R[1]	1937-1940	27 (13)	Wright	420	hp
D17W	1937	1	P & W	600	hp
D17A[1]	1939-1940	9 (1)	Wright	350	hp
E17B[1]	1937-1940	48 (31)	Jacobs	285	hp
SE17B	1937-1939	4	Jacobs	285	hp
E17L	1937	1	Jacobs	225	hp
F17D[1]	1938-1942	59 (38)	Jacobs	330	hp
G17S	1946-1948	16	P & W	450	hp

[1] Procured for use of Army and/or Navy and designated UC-43 or YC-43 (Army) and GB-1 or GB-2 (Navy).

[2] Figures in parenthesis indicate total military purchase.

LOWER HORSEPOWER STAGGERWINGS, PERFORMANCE & SPECIFICATIONS

Model	B17L	E17B	F17D
Top speed	175	195	195
Cruising speed	152	177	182
Landing speed	45	45	46
Rate of climb	1,000	1,200	1,300
Service ceiling	15,000	18,000	18,000
Range	500-850	700	750
Wing span	32	32	32
Wing area	273	296	296
Gross weight	3,150	3,350	3,550
Empty weight	1,800	2,080	2,155
Wing loading	11.5	11.3	11.97
Power loading	14	11.8	10.75
Fuel capacity	50	77	76
Oil capacity	5	5	5
Horsepower	225	285	330
Propeller	Hartzell	Curtiss	Hamilton

3. Beechcraft T-34 Mentor, Model 45

A TOTAL OF 1,904 Beechcraft T-34 Mentors were produced from 1948 to 1958 inclusive. The Air Force took delivery of 353 Mentors between March, 1950, and October, 1956; the Navy bought 423, delivered between October, 1954, and July, 1957. Beech built an additional 318 units for export (the plane received a CAA type certificate in October, 1953); and the balance were constructed under license in Canada, Japan, and Argentina.

The Mentor was a Beech gamble, designed and financed with Beech funds. The prototype was test-flown December 2, 1948, and

Beechcraft T-34A, powered with a 225 hp Continental engine is Bonanza kissin' cousin. Top speed: 189 mph; cruise 173 mph; fully aerobatic except for inverted spins.

contained a substantial amount of Bonanza airframe. The original was fitted with a Continental E-185 engine. It had a cruise of 160 mph at 10,000 feet, top speed of 176 mph, service ceiling of 18,000 feet, and a gross weight of 2,650 lbs. It was stressed for 10 positive and 4.5 negative G's, and was fully aerobatic.

Mentor production actually began for the military in 1953 after a leisurely evaluation by the Air Force and Navy. Air Force models were the YT-34, powered with the Continental E-225–8 engine of 220 hp, and the T-34A, fitted with the Continental 0–470–13, rated at 225 hp. The Navy Mentor, T-34B, had the 0–470–13 engine, and was distinguishable from the T-34A chiefly by its yellow paint and the elimination of the wedge-shaped fairing between the bottom of the rudder and the fuselage.

Although the Mentor seems an ideal sport plane, few have found their way into private hands. After many thousands of hours as a combination primary/basic trainer, many T-34's were junked by the military. Something over a hundred of them were given to the fortunate Civil Air Patrol. Still others went to Air Force Base flying clubs. Most of the CAP and flying club Mentors were still in use as the sixties drew to a close, and about a hundred remained in Navy service at Pensacola.

Our personal experience with the T-34 is limited to a couple of rear-seat guest flights courtesy of the Sheppard AFB Flying Club several years ago, plus some annual inspections and minor service work done in our shops (we operated an airport at the time) on Mentors from the Altus AFB Flying Club.

The airplane is easy to handle on the ground, visibility is ex-

Navy version is T-34B; same engine and performance as Air Force trainer. Navy Mentor lacked wedged fairing between bottom of rudder and fuselage tail cone.

cellent, and taxiing is effortless. Throttle, prop, and mixture controls are on a quadrant mounted on the left side of the fuselage, and of course, you have a stick control instead of a wheel. The rear cockpit has a complete set of instruments, dual controls; in fact, everything found in front except, perhaps, the inverter switch that controls the electric compass and attitude gyros.

The T-34 takes off like a Bonanza, though riding in the center of the airplane and using stick control makes it seem like a hotter military type. Full throttle (2,600 rpm) with prop in full low pitch and mixture full rich quickly swings the air-speed needle through 60 knots (69 mph) at which point you lighten the nose wheel and are airborne. Standard climb procedure is to keep the throttle wide open but reduce rpms to about 2,350 or 2,400 with the prop control and adjust air speed to 100 knots (115 mph). These settings produced a climb-rate of 900 fpm which fell off very little, on a hot day, to 4,000 feet, where we trimmed for cruise.

Stalls were gentle, preceded by some aerodynamic buffeting. With power, indicating 53 knots (60 mph), gear and flaps up, the nose dropped while the plane continued to shake a little. Power off and clean the stall came at 58 knots (67 mph) IAS. Gear and flaps down with power off, she quit at 46 knots (53 mph).

At 6,500 ft, pulling 23 inches and 2,100 rpms, we indicated 135 knots which worked out to 153 knots true, or about 175 mph. Fuel consumption at 65% power at 6,500 is about 10 gph.

The Mentor lands much like a Bonanza, although it seemed to us that the Air Force figures were all on the high side: 90 knots (104 mph) downwind; 80 knots on base leg (92 mph); 75 knots (86 mph) on final and 60 knots (70 mph) at touchdown.

T-34 PERFORMANCE AND SPECIFICATIONS

Engine: Continental 0–470–13, rated at 225 hp at 2,600 rpms

Top speed	189 mph
Best cruise	173 mph
Service ceiling	19,500 ft
Gross weight	2,950 lbs
Wing span	32 ft 10 in
Length	25 ft., 11 in
Height	9 ft., 7 in.
Wing loading	16.03 lbs/sq ft
Power loading	12.89 lbs/hp

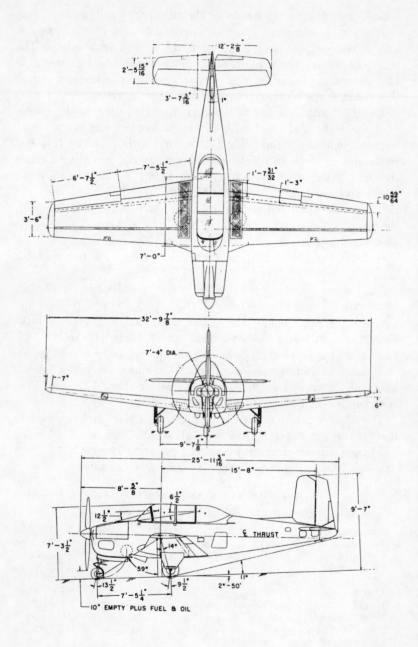

10" EMPTY PLUS FUEL & OIL

4. Beechcraft Musketeers

ACTUALLY, Beech offers five Musketeers (despite company ads which play the "Three Musketeers" bit to a belated death). All possess the same basic airframe and were developed from the Model 23 Musketeer that first appeared in 1962.

The 1969 Musketeer Series consisted of the 200 hp Super III, a four-placer with standard avionics priced at $18,450; the 180 hp Custom III, a four-placer selling for $16,950; the Custom III Aerobatic at $18,950; the two-place (four-place optional) Sport III of 150 hp at $14,250; and the two-place (four-place optional) Sport III Aerobatic which was priced at $16,250.

It's worth noting that Beech has held the price line against inflation pretty well with the Musketeer. The first Model 23 was priced at $13,300 back in January of 1962, and it was originally certified with a 160 hp Lycoming.

We were introduced to the first Musketeer by Miss Joyce Case (three times Women's National Aerobatic Champion, now with Cessna), and Joyce in turn took us to John I. Elliot, chief project engineer for the Musketeer. We asked John, an unflappable, pipe-smoking type in his forties, just how Beech had approached the design of a new economy aircraft in the single-engine lightplane market.

He measured us calmly. "When our engineering task force was handed this job," he said, "we knew we'd have to do several things to meet the challenge successfully. It called for new manufacturing methods and new materials; a minimum number of parts and simplified assembly.

"Fortunately," he went on, "we possessed both equipment and experience for working with the revolutionary new truss-grid, honeycomb-core type construction. This stemmed from our sub-contract to make airfoil surfaces for Convair's F-106 supersonic fighter; we used this same method of construction in the Musket-

Musketeer II, which appeared in mid-1964; is powered with Continental 165 hp fuel-injected engine. Top speed, 146 mph; cruise 137.

eer's wings. Result: less weight, greater strength, smoother skin, fewer parts, and lower cost. It's the first time truss-grid members have been employed in a sport/trainer/business plane."

"It's a laminar flow wing, isn't it?"

"Yes," John replied, "and each wing has two degrees of twist so that the tips will stall last. This makes for a combination that is efficient at higher speeds, yet provides docile stall characteristics."

Joyce returned with a Musketeer wing rib. It looked as if it had been cut from the radiator of a Model A Ford—except that the stuff was aluminum. "The wing ribs are sawed from sheets of this honeycomb 'sandwich,'" she said, handing it to us. And we were amazed at its extremely light weight. It was also far stronger than any wing rib we had ever seen.

"This also allows us to eliminate rivets over most of the wing's surface," John said. "The skin is bonded to the ribs, and that gives us a very smooth outer surface.

"Each wing has a single spar which passes through the side of the fuselage and joins in the center with bridge-type connection plates at top and bottom. In addition, there are wing-shear bolts secured to fittings on each side of the fuselage. So, here again we obtained unusual strength with less weight and lowered costs— in this case because we eliminated a center section carry-through structure.

"We've really tested the pants off this wing, been very rough with it," John concluded with a trace of pride. "For example, we gave it a vibration test equal to a hundred years of normal operation at full gross load."

"How about the fuselage," we inquired. "Is it conventional in construction?"

"Not exactly. The fuselage does employ bulkheads, but the skin, with few exceptions, provides its own stringers. We accomplished this by putting a 90-degree bend in the skins at the skin splice."

The Model 23's project engineer then went on to explain the plane's tail surfaces. The Musketeer has an all-movable horizontal tail plane called a "stabilator." There is no elevator or fixed horizontal stabilizer. (Piper also uses this so-called "flying tail," as does the Cessna Cardinal.) The Musketeer's stabilator has a large trim and anti-servo tab. For every degree of deflection of

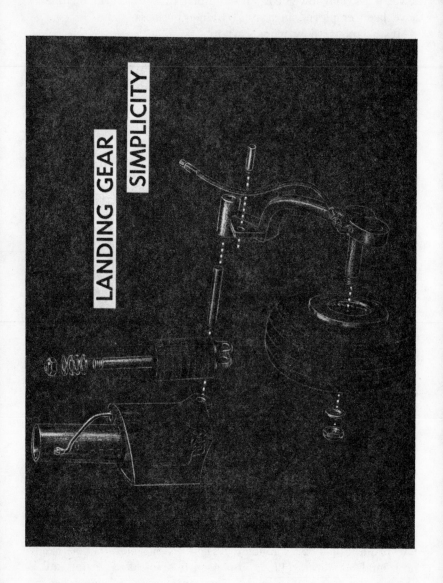

LANDING GEAR SIMPLICITY

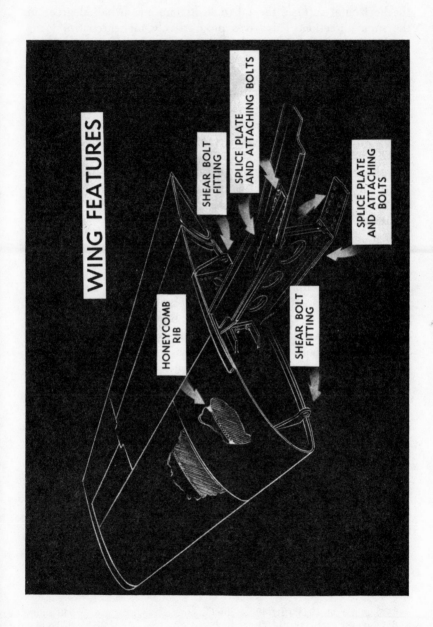

WING FEATURES

HONEYCOMB RIB

SHEAR BOLT FITTING

SPLICE PLATE AND ATTACHING BOLTS

SPLICE PLATE AND ATTACHING BOLTS

SHEAR BOLT FITTING

the horizontal surface, the tab deflects one and a half degrees in the same direction. This gives progressively higher control loads as the stabilator is deflected from trim position—a situation that seems desirable in normal flight operations, but which is less than desirable for vertical maneuvers in aerobatic flight. As ever in airplane design, to get something you have to give something.

The Musketeer's landing gear is about as simple and practical as a landing gear can get on a modern low-wing airplane, and needs almost no maintenance. It consists of a cast strut housing, a rubber-in-compression shock absorber, and an articulated strut. John said that an articulated strut has very little rebound to it, which means that it should smooth out the landings of even the beginning student. Another feature is that all three units are identical—including tire and wheel size—for maximum interchangeability of parts.

The Musketeer has a 141-inch wheel tread which translates into excellent ground control. "We did considerable drop-testing with this gear," John told us, "and determined that the design loads will never exceed a limit of 3.2 G's. That makes us very enthusiastic over this rubber-in-compression shock absorber."

Another noteworthy feature of the Musketeer is that its power-plant package bolts onto the plane as a separate subassembly. Everything from the firewall forward comes off by removal of only four bolts. This simplifies maintenance—and of course made it easy for Beech to install other engines for the planned expansion of the Musketeer Series.

MUSKETEER MODEL 23 (1962) PERFORMANCE & SPECIFICATIONS

Engine: Lycoming 0–320-D2B rated at 160 hp at 2,700 rpm

Performance

High speed (sea level, at 2,700 rpm)	144 mph
Cruise, 75% power at 7,000 ft.	135 mph
Cruise, 65% power at 10,000 ft	128 mph
Stall speed, 30 degrees flaps	62 mph
Stall speed, flaps up	70 mph
Flap extension speed (max.)	110 mph

Range

65% power at 10,000 ft, 40 gal fuel	549 miles
65% power at 10,000 ft, 60 gal fuel	873 miles

75% power at 7,000 ft, 40 gal fuel .... 507 miles
75% power at 7,000 ft, 60 gal fuel .... 803 miles

(above figures include warm-up, taxi, climb to altitude and 45-minute reserve)

Rate of climb .... 710 fpm
Service ceiling .... 13,500 ft
Take-off distance (over 50-foot obstacle) .... 1,420 ft

Model 23 Musketeer is licensed in normal category at maximum gross weight of 2,300 lbs; in utility category at a gross of 1,960 lbs.

Specifications

Gross weight .... 2,300 lbs
Empty weight .... 1,250 lbs
Standard equipment empty weight .... 1,300 lbs
Standard useful load with 40 gal fuel .... 1,000 lbs
Wing area .... 145 sq ft
Wing loading at gross weight .... 15.86 lbs/sq ft
Power loading at gross weight .... 14.38 lbs per hp
Wing span .... 32.75 ft
Chord .... 52.73 in
Length .... 25 ft
Height (top of rudder) .... 8.25 ft
Cabin length .... 7.8 ft
Cabin width .... 3.4 ft
Baggage capacity .... 140 lbs
Standard fuel capacity .... 38.8 gal usable
Standard maximum fuel capacity .... 58.8 gal usable
Oil capacity .... 8 quarts

MUSKETEER II (1964)

The Musketeer II, first shown in mid-June, 1964, had three principal refinements: a new fuel-injected engine, additional rear windows, and an increase in price.

The interior cabin appointments were also luxuried-up a bit. Visibility was improved with addition of two rear windows, and the new Continental 165 hp engine with fuel injection added slightly to performance. Factory list price of the Musketeer II was $14,250 at the time of its introduction.

Sales of the original Model 23 had been disappointing to Beech and a mystery to us—and no one seemed to know the trouble. The airplane was as honest as advertised; would do everything Beech claimed and was fun to fly. And $13,300 seemed cheap enough considering that this price included avionics and other

35

features usually costing extra. So, where had Beech missed the mark?

Slowly, the answer seeped through: Beech had simply failed to "sell" the Musketeer to Beech dealers. Salesmen accustomed to demonstrating Bonanzas and Barons and Queen Airs found it hard to generate a lot of enthusiasm for an economy craft that climbed 750 fpm and trued-out slightly above 130 mph. It was like asking Cadillac salesmen to sell Corvairs.

There were undoubtedly other reasons for the Musketeer's slow start, including the obvious fact that Beech had never sold to this segment of the market before; nevertheless, this fine four-placer (and all Musketeers of 160 hp and above are true four-place airplanes; you don't have to empty your pockets to get it off the ground with four big people and enough gas to get where you're going) was slow to make a dent in a market traditionally dominated by Cessna and Piper.

Specifications and performance figures were not much changed by appearance of the Musketeer II with its extra five horsepower and fuel injection, as the following figures will reveal:

Gross weight	2,350 lbs
Empty weight	1,398 lbs
Useful load	952 lbs
Top speed at sea level	146 mph
Maximum cruise speed (75% power @ 7,000 ft)	137 mph
Range, with 45 min. reserve (55% power, 60 gal)	906 mi
Rate of climb at sea level	770 fpm
Service ceiling	12,550 ft

MUSKETEER SPORT III, CUSTOM III & SUPER III

In October, 1965, Beech announced the Series III Musketeer in three models: the 150 hp two-place Sport III at $11,500; the 165 hp four-place Custom III at $14,950, and the 200 hp Super III four-placer with a price tag of $16,350.

With minor refinements, these three craft continued in production through 1969. By the end of July, 1967, more than 1,550 Musketeers had been produced (1,000 of these at Beech's Liberal, Kansas, Division) and the design well established.

In 1968, Beech introduced the aerobatic version of the Musketeer Sport III, and in 1969 offered an aerobatic version of the Custom III, by which time the Custom had a 180 hp engine.

Musketeer Sport III fitted for aerobatics is capable of satisfying most pilots who aerobat for sport. Engine is 150 hp Lycoming. Top speed, 140 mph. Two-place.

During one of our regular trips to Wichita in which we make the rounds of the various aeronautical watering holes, Beech's press relations man, Vern Modeland, mentioned that an aerobatic Sport III demonstrator was available if we'd care to "fling it around a little."

This called for some fast thinking. We could either admit our incompetence at such activity, or find a graceful way to weasel out of it. Naturally, we chose the latter course. "Vern," we said seriously, "there's nothing I'd like better. However, I'm sure the average flyer would rather have a report on this plane by a champion aerobatic pilot. Why don't we ask Harold Krier to wring it out and give *his* opinion?"

"Good idea," Vern agreed.

Harold was amenable, provided he be allowed to keep the plane for several days in order to really become acquainted with it. That was okay with Beech. So, we occupied ourselves with other business and returned to Krier at the end of the week for his evaluation of the Aerobatic Sport III.

"Well, I like this airplane," Harold began. "It's a fun machine with class. I've put about five hours on the recording tach, almost all of that in akro-flight. Judging it purely as an aerobatic machine, however, I have to say there are a couple of things about it I don't like."

Neat panel of Aerobatic Sport III. G-meter is at lower right of T-grouped flight instruments.

"For an instance?"

"Control loads in vertical maneuvers. You have to work at it to do a good inside loop in this airplane. Because of the heavy stabilator force you need two hands on the wheel; and you need another hand for power management because the Musketeer has a fixed-pitch prop, and you must back off power as you dive for speed to begin the loop or your rpms will overrun the red line. During the pull-up you need both hands on the wheel even though you have already thumbed the electric trim button for nose-up attitude, because the electric trim does not act instantaneously. Then, you apply power again, and hold the wheel hard back as you arc upward. As it swings over the top throttle again it must be retarded to prevent engine overspeed.

"Now, I realize I'm finding fault strictly from an aerobatic pilot's point of view, and Beech did not design the Musketeer to please us tumble-types. The airplane is, as Beech says, a sport/trainer with fair crosscountry ability and limited aerobatic potential. I'm sure they could speed up the electric trim and perhaps modify the stabilator/anti-servo action to make vertical maneuvers real easy; but of course that would detract from other desirable and more constantly employed traits.

"Anyway, after a little practice, you can do very good loops, and do them with no altitude loss.

"The Musketeer's spin characteristics are very good. She won't spin accidentally—that is, you must hold her in a spin with ailerons *against* the direction of rotation. Turn loose of the controls, and rotation stops within half a turn. She spins equally well in either direction, and control response is so effective that you'll get a pronounced jolt if you use full controls for recovery.

"Snap rolls are good using an entry speed of 85 mph. The owner's manual says 100 mph; but you won't get her to break clean at that speed. But she'll do real neat snaps at 85 mph if you'll come all the way back on the wheel and use rudder only, no aileron.

"The Sport III did nice Immelmanns for me, with about 300 to 400 feet of altitude gain, although I had to disagree with the owner's manual again. It said 150 mph entry speed, while 140 mph produced a much better maneuver. I performed Immelmanns to both left and right.

"I also did a lot of aileron rolls because the Musketeer's ailerons are so good that this maneuver is pure fun. Four-point rolls (without power) are good.

"You can't do any outside maneuvers in this plane because of limited forward control travel, and she won't spin inverted for the same reason; most I could get out of it was an inverted spiral. She does, however, make nice inverted gliding turns holding 85 mph.

"Just for rocks, I planned a short airshow-type routine, within the limits of the Musketeer's aerobatic ability, and flew it. I began with a four-point roll, pulled up into a half-roll on a 45 degree

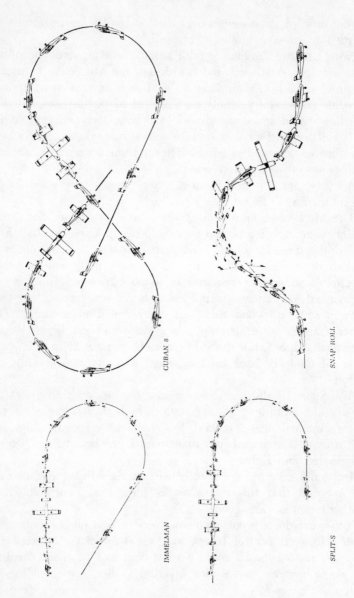

CUBAN 8

SNAP ROLL

IMMELMAN

SPLIT-S

Typical aerobatic maneuvers you can perform in the
Aerobatic Musketeer Sport III.

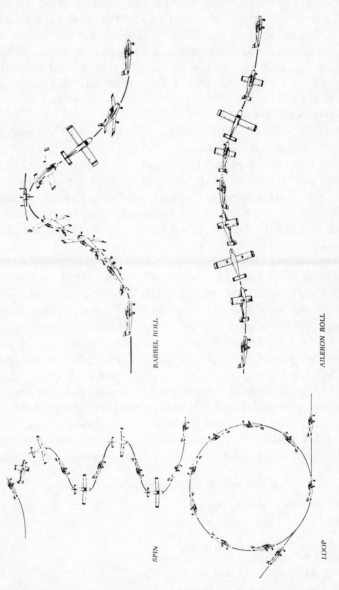

BARREL ROLL.

AILERON ROLL.

SPIN

LOOP

Sport III owner's manual says you'll lose 100 feet of altitude in loop, but check-pilot Hal Krier found no altitude loss necessary. Krier reports aileron rolls easy and fun in Musketeer.

climbing line. Split-essing out of that from inverted attitude, I did a snap roll on top of a loop and let that lead me into a chandelle. I spun off the chandelle and allowed that to take me into a Cuban 8. Next, an Immelmann, a snap roll on a descending 45 degree line, followed by two inside slow rolls around a 180 degree turn. Then I concluded with a slow, slow roll. Obviously, a guy has enough options with this craft to perform some very respectable amateur aerobatics."

And there you have the opinion of three-time National Aerobatic Champion Harold Krier.

The Sport III is roomy inside and has excellent sound-proofing (Krier commented on both features). Behind the two front seats is a large space ending at the rear bulkhead. This area holds 340 pounds of baggage for normal operation, or an optional rear seat. With four aboard, however, fuel is cut to 28.8 gallons and baggage to a lightweight shaving kit.

Standard equipment includes a 90-channel transceiver (actually, 90 channels to talk, 100 to receive), with OMNI and Localizer built in. The aerobatic version differs from the standard Sport III only superficially. The Akro model has a G-meter in the instrument panel, quick-release right-hand door, shoulder harness for two front seats; checkered stripes on wings and rudder, and a placard to remind you of the craft's limitations. This plane is certified for limited aerobatics under Part 3 of the FAR at utility category gross of 2,030 pounds, and licensed for normal operation for a gross of 2,250 pounds. The Sport III is quickly distinguishable from the Custom III and Super III because it retains the two windows on each side that this airframe started out with, while the Custom and Super (and Musketeer II) have three windows on each side.

MUSKETEER SPORT III ESTIMATED OPERATING COSTS

Direct operating costs per hour

Gasoline	$2.96
Oil	.18
Inspection, maintenance & prop overhaul	1.22
Engine overhaul allowance	.81
Total direct operating costs per hour	$5.17

Indirect operating costs per hour

Hangar rent	$1.05
Insurance	1.71
Total indirect operating cost per hour	$2.76

Total operating cost per hour $7.93
Operating cost per mile .... .064
Cost per seat mile (2 seats) .... .032

Fuel consumption based on operation at 65% power with allowance for warm-up, taxi and climb. Computed at 7.8 gph at 38¢ gal, and assuming aircraft utilization of 400 hours (49,200 miles) per year. Engine overhaul is assumed at 1,500 hours; hangar rental is based on national average of $420 per year. Insurance includes hull and public liability (100,000/300,000), passenger liability (100,000 for 1 seat), and property damage (100,000). Rate based on one-year policy obtainable under Beech finance plans.

MUSKETEER SPORT III PERFORMANCE AND SPECIFICATIONS

Engine: Lycoming 0–320-E2C rated at 150 horsepower at 2,700 rpm for all operations.

Performance

Maximum speed: Sea level at 2,700 rpm .... 122 knots/140 mph

Cruising speeds:
    75% power at 7,000 feet .... 114 knots/131 mph
    65% power at 10,000 feet .... 107 knots/123 mph
    55% power at 10,000 feet .... 98 knots/113 mph

Rate of climb: (sea level)
    2,250 pounds .... 700 feet per minute
    2,030 pounds .... 900 feet per minute

Service ceiling:
    2,250 pounds .... 11,100 feet
    2,030 pounds .... 14,900 feet

Absolute ceiling:
    2,250 pounds .... 12,950 feet
    2,030 pounds .... 16,700 feet

Stall speed: Zero thrust, flaps 35 degrees .... 49 knots/56 mph

Take-off distance: (flaps 15 degrees)
    Ground run (2,250 pounds) .... 885 feet
    Total over 50-foot-high obstacle (2,250 pounds) .... 1,320 feet
    Ground run (2,030 pounds) .... 685 feet
    Total over 50-foot-high obstacles (2,030 pounds) .... 1,033 feet

Landing distance: (flaps 35 degrees)
    Ground run (2,250 pounds) .... 590 feet
    Total over 50-foot-high obstacle (2,250 pounds) .... 1,220 feet
    Ground run (2,030 pounds) .... 570 feet
    Total over 50-foot-high obstacle (2,030 pounds) .... 1,190 feet

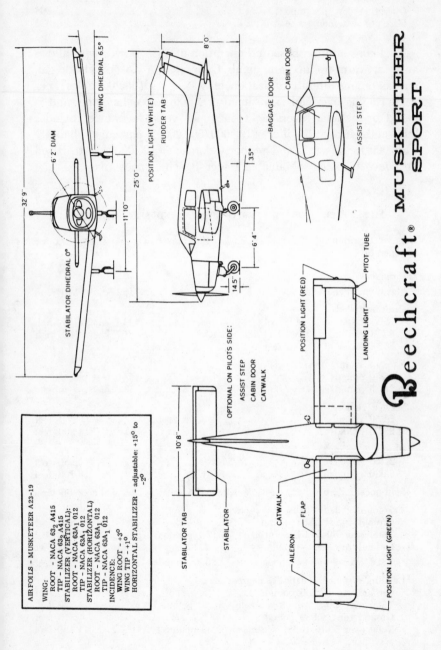

AIRFOILS - MUSKETEER A23-19

WING:
ROOT - NACA 63_2 A415
TIP - NACA 63_2 A415
STABILIZER (VERTICAL):
ROOT - NACA $63A_1$ 012
TIP - NACA $63A_1$ 012
STABILIZER (HORIZONTAL)
ROOT - NACA $63A_1$ 012
TIP - NACA $63A_1$ 012
INCIDENCE:
WING ROOT - $+3^o$
WING TIP - $+1^o$
HORIZONTAL STABILIZER - adjustable: $+15^o$ to -2°

WING DIHEDRAL 6.5°

STABILATOR DIHEDRAL 0°

6' 2" DIAM

32' 9"

25' 0"

11' 10"

8' 0"

35°

6' 4"

14.5"

POSITION LIGHT (WHITE)

RUDDER TAB

BAGGAGE DOOR

CABIN DOOR

ASSIST STEP

OPTIONAL ON PILOTS SIDE:
ASSIST STEP
CABIN DOOR
CATWALK

10' 8"

STABILATOR TAB

STABILATOR

POSITION LIGHT (RED)

PITOT TUBE

LANDING LIGHT

AILERON

FLAP

CATWALK

POSITION LIGHT (GREEN)

ℬeechcraft® MUSKETEER SPORT

44

Range: Includes warm-up, taxi, take-off and climb to altitude with 45-minute reserve. Reserve computed at 55% power.

75% power @ 7,000 feet	767 miles on 58.8 gallons
	475 miles on 38.8 gallons
	331 miles on 28.8 gallons
65% power @ 10,000 feet	827 miles on 58.8 gallons
	511 miles on 38.8 gallons
	354 miles on 28.8 gallons
55% power @ 10,000 feet	883 miles on 58.8 gallons
	546 miles on 38.8 gallons
	377 miles on 28.8 gallons

Weights
Gross weight utility category .... 2,030 pounds
Gross weight normal category .... 2,250 pounds
Empty weight (dry) .... 1,350 pounds
Useful load normal category .... 900 pounds
Useful load breakdown:
   Oil, fuel (58.8 usable), 2 people, 185 pounds baggage
   Oil, fuel (38.8 usable), 2 people, 305 pounds baggage
   Oil, fuel (28.8 usable), 4 people, 25 pounds baggage
Baggage .... 340 pounds

Areas
Wing .... 146.00 square feet

Dimensions
Wing span .... 32 feet, 9 inches
Length .... 25 feet, 0 inches
Height .... 8 feet, 3 inches
Cabin length (instrument panel aft) .... 71 inches
Cabin width .... 41 inches
Headroom (seat to ceiling)
   Front seat .... 39.25 inches
   Rear seat (optional) .... 38 inches
Baggage door size .... 18.5 by 23.75 inches
Cabin door size .... 38 by 40 inches

Technical Data
Wing loading:
   Utility category .... 13.90 lbs per sq ft
   Normal category .... 15.41 lbs per sq ft
Power loading:
   Utility category .... 13.53 pounds per hp
   Normal category .... 15.00 pounds per hp
Compartment volume:
   Baggage .... 28.8 cubic feet
Fuel capacity:
   Fuel 60 gallons .... 58.8 usable
   Oil 2 gallons .... 1.5 usable
Fuel specifications:
   Fuel 80/87

45

Landing gear:

Brakes .... Hydraulic disc
Main wheel tire size .... 6.00–6 by 15
Nose wheel tire size .... 6.00–6 by 15

MUSKETEER CUSTOM III PERFORMANCE & SPECIFICATIONS
(1966 MODEL, 165 HP)

Engine: Continental 10–346A, fuel injected, rated at 165 hp at 2,700 rpms

Top speed at sea level (2,700 rpm) .... 146 mph
Best cruise speed, 75% power at 7,000 ft .... 137 mph
Cruising range, 75% power at 7,000 ft .... 778 mi
Rate of climb (initial) .... 725 fpm
Service ceiling .... 11,870 ft
Gross weight .... 2,400 lbs
Useful load .... 1,025 lbs
Wing span .... 32 ft, 9 in
Length .... 25 ft
Height .... 8 ft, 3 in
Wing area .... 146 sq ft
Wing loading (gross) .... 16.10 lbs/sq ft
Power loading (gross, normal category) .... 14.25 lbs/hp
Standard fuel capacity .... 60 gal
Oil capacity .... 8 qts
Cabin length .... 94 in
Cabin height .... 48.5 in
Cabin width .... 41 in

MUSKETEER CUSTOM III (1968–1969 MODEL, 180 HP)

The following operating costs assume 400 hours (53,600 mi) per year aircraft utilization. Gasoline consumption is figured at 65% power, allowing for warm-up, taxi and climb, and computed at 9 gph, at 42¢ per gal. Engine overhaul allowance is based

Musketeer Custom III is four-to-six-place; 180 Lycoming engine. Top speed, 151 mph. Range with reserves, 860 miles.

on expected overhaul at 1,500 hours, and hangar rental is figured at $420 per year. Insurance, based on one-year policies obtainable under Beech finance plans, includes hull and public liability (100,000/300,000), passenger liability for three seats (100,000/300,000), and property damage (100,000). This includes all risk and crash, ground and flight coverage, for pleasure, business and industrial aid use, flown by named private or commercial pilot. Operation cost per mile is based on 134 mph speed.

Direct operating costs per hour
Gasoline $3.78
Oil .... .18
Inspection, maintenance & prop overhaul 1.22
Engine overhaul allowance 1.14

Total direct operating cost per hour $6.32

Indirect operating costs per hour
Hangar rental $1.05
Insurance 2.17

Total indirect operating cost per hour $3.22
Total operating cost per hour $9.54
Operating cost per mile .... .071
Cost per seat mile (4 seats) .... .081

MUSKETEER CUSTOM III (1968–1969) PERFORMANCE & SPECIFICATIONS

Engine: Lycoming 0–360-A2G four-cylinder fuel injection engine rated 180 horsepower at 2,700 rpm for all operations

Performance
Maximum speed: 2,700 rpm at sea level .... 126 knots/151 mph
Cruising speeds:
   75% power at 7,000 feet .... 124 knots/143 mph
   65% power at 10,000 feet .... 116 knots/134 mph
   55% power at 10,000 feet .... 107 knots/123 mph
Rate of climb: Sea level
   Full throttle, gross weight .... 820 feet per minute
Service ceiling .... 13,650 feet
Absolute ceiling .... 15,500 feet
Stall speed: Zero thrust, flaps 35 degrees .... 52 knots/59 mph
Take-off distance: (Flaps 15 degrees)
   Ground run .... 950 feet
   Total over 50-foot obstacle .... 1,380 feet
Landing distance: (flaps 35 degrees)
   Ground run .... 640 feet
   Total over 50-foot obstacle .... 1,275 feet

Range: Includes warm-up, taxi, takeoff and climb to altitude and 45-minute reserve. Reserve computed at 55% power.

75% power at 7,500 feet	685 miles on 58.8 gallons
	420 miles on 38.8 gallons
	285 miles on 28.8 gallons
65% power at 10,500 feet	780 miles on 58.8 gallons
	465 miles on 38.8 gallons
	308 miles on 28.8 gallons
55% power at 10,500 feet	860 miles on 58.8 gallons
	505 miles on 38.8 gallons
	331 miles on 28.8 gallons

Weights

Gross weight utility category .... 2,030 pounds
Gross weight normal category .... 2,450 pounds
Empty weight (dry) .... 1,375 pounds
Useful load normal category .... 1,085 pounds

Useful load breakdown:
    Oil, fuel (28.8 usable), 4 people, 210 pounds baggage
    Oil, fuel (38.8 usable), 4 people, 150 pounds baggage
    Oil, fuel (58.8 usable), 3 people, 200 pounds baggage
    Baggage .... 270 pounds

Areas

Wing .... 146.00 square feet

Dimensions

Wing span .... 32 feet, 9 inches
Length .... 25 feet, 0 inches
Height .... 8 feet, 3 inches
Cabin length (instrument panel aft) .... 95 inches
Cabin width .... 41 inches
Headroom (seat to ceiling)
    Front seat .... 39.25 inches
    Rear seat .... 37.75 inches
Baggage door size .... 18.5 by 23.75 inches
Cabin door size .... 38 by 40 inches

Technical data

Wing loading at gross weight normal
    category .... 16.78 pounds per square foot
Power loading at gross weight normal
    category .... 13.61 pounds per horsepower
Compartment volume:
    Baggage .... 19.5 cubic feet
    Hat shelf .... 3.8 cubic feet
Fuel capacity:
    Fuel 60 gallons .... 58.8 usable
    Oil 2 gallons .... 1.5 usable
Fuel specifications:
    Fuel .... 100/130 octane

Landing gear:
Brakes .... Hydraulic disc
Main wheel tire size .... 6.00–6 by 15
Nose wheel tire size .... 6.00–6 by 15

MUSKETEER SUPER III

The 1969 Musketeer Super (and the 1968 and 1967 Super) has the same brakes as the Bonanza, a definite improvement, as well as an optional left door, in addition to the right-hand cabin door. A constant speed prop is also available for an extra $975; however, this item adds little to take-off and climb and almost nothing to cruising speeds. It is probably not worth the extra money on this airplane except for unimproved strips of high elevation.

Musketeer Super III, four-to-six-placer, powered with 200 hp Lycoming engine. Top speed, 158 mph; range, with reserves, 823 miles.

At 7,500 ft, the Super we flew (fixed-pitch prop) trued-out at 145 mph with 75% power. 65% power produced 140 mph TAS. We were well under gross, with just two aboard and no baggage, and it was a hot summer day—92 degrees F on the surface—and take-off required just 11 seconds. Climb, at 95 IAS, gave us 900 fpm.

At 60 mph indicated, control was solid and turns normal. We tried stalls, and with flaps down, power on, the break came at 50 mph. With power off and flaps down she quit flying at 57 mph. In each case the stall was gentle and altitude loss did not exceed 175 ft.

Optional left-hand door on Musketeer simplifies passenger entrance and exit, and is considered a safety feature by some buyers.

Then we went to 9,500 ft (temperature-corrected for a density altitude of 11,500) where the air speed indicated 123 mph. We pushed the buttons of our genuine aviator's chronograph over some section lines below (which in this part of the country are surveyed exactly one mile apart), and averaged the results after making a 180 and flying a reciprocal heading over the same ground. It gave us a ground speed of 144 mph. We had 62% power at this altitude according to the numbers.

The Musketeers are very stable airplanes—you tend to do a lot of flying with trim alone. Visibility is very good, including downward, because you sit ahead of the wing's leading edge, or almost so. These are roomy, plush and quiet airplanes inside, and the traditional Beechcraft quality is evident throughout. Controls are interconnected on the Super and Custom. On the Sport III rudder and aileron are independent.

The Musketeer nose wheel (originally full-swivelling) is steerable with the rudder pedals 15 degrees each way. A shimmy dampener was added to this wheel early in Musketeer production. So, this airplane handles very nicely on the ground.

MUSKETEER SUPER III OPERATING COSTS

Direct operating costs per hour

Gasoline $3.95
Oil .... .18
Inspection, maintenance & prop overhaul 1.22
Engine overhaul allowance (at 1,200 hours) 1.27

Total direct operating cost per hour $6.62

Indirect operating costs per hour

Hangar rental $1.05
Insurance $2.32

Total indirect operating cost per hour $3.37
Total operating cost per hour $9.99
Operating cost per mile .... .071
Total cost per seat mile (four seats) .... .018

Above figures are based on aircraft utilization of 400 hours (56,400 miles) per year. Fuel consumption is figured at 65% power, allowing for warm-up, taxi and climb, at 9.4 gph and 42¢ per gallon. Engine overhaul is assumed at 1,200 hours and hangar rent at the national average of $420 per year. Insurance includes hull and public liability (100,000/300,000), passenger liability for 3 seats (100,000/300,000), and property damage (100,000). Includes all risk and crash, ground and flight coverage, for business, pleasure and industrial aid use, flown by named private or commercial pilot. Annual premium based on airplane evaluation of $18,450 at a rate obtainable under Beech finance plans.

We note that engine overhaul is given at 1,200 hours on the Super Musketeer and at 1,500 hours on the Custom; but according to Beech this raises the direct operating cost only 13¢ per hour. If this is true, we're missing something somewhere in our arithmetic.

Beechcraft Financing of the Super III. Assuming a purchase price of $18,450 of a new Super III, a 25% down payment of $4,612 will result in an average monthly payment of $425.

Beech also has a number of leasing plans available for Musketeer acquisition.

Musketeer Super III instrument panel. Auto pilot at lower right. This well-equipped craft went to Sweden.

MUSKETEER SUPER III PERFORMANCE AND SPECIFICATIONS

Engines: Lycoming four-cylinder, 10–360-A2B, fuel injection engine rated at 200 horsepower at 2,700 rpm for all operations.

Performance

Maximum speed: 2,700 rpm at sea level .... 137 knots/158 mph
Cruising speeds:
   75% power at 7,000 feet .... 130 knots/150 mph
   65% power at 10,000 feet .... 122 knots/141 mph
   55% power at 10,000 feet .... 114 knots/132 mph
Rate of climb: Full throttle, gross weight .... 880 feet per minute
Service ceiling .... 14,850 feet
Absolute ceiling .... 16,750 feet
Stall speed: Zero thrust, flaps 35 degrees .... 53 knots/61 mph
Take-off distance: (flaps 15 degrees)
   Ground run .... 950 feet
   Total over 50-foot-high obstacle .... 1,380 feet
Landing distance: (flaps 35 degrees)
   Ground run .... 660 feet
   Total over 50-foot-high obstacle .... 1,300 feet

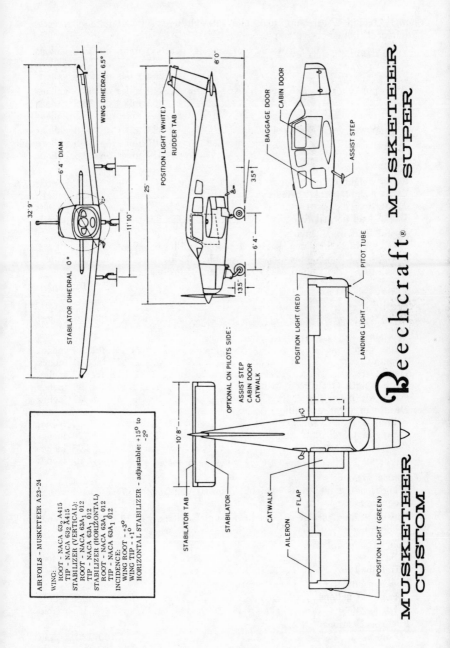

AIR FOILS - MUSKETEER A23-24

WING:
  ROOT - NACA 63₂A415
  TIP - NACA 63₂A415
STABILIZER (VERTICAL):
  ROOT - NACA 63A₁012
  TIP - NACA 63A₁012
STABILIZER (HORIZONTAL)
  ROOT - NACA 63A₁012
  TIP - NACA 63A₁012
INCIDENCE:
  WING ROOT - +3°
  WING TIP - +1°
  HORIZONTAL STABILIZER - adjustable: +15° to -2°

32' 9"

WING DIHEDRAL 6.5°

6' 4" DIAM

STABILATOR DIHEDRAL 0°

11' 10"

25'

POSITION LIGHT (WHITE)
RUDDER TAB

8' 0"

3.5°

6' 4"

13.5°

BAGGAGE DOOR
CABIN DOOR
ASSIST STEP

OPTIONAL ON PILOTS SIDE:
  ASSIST STEP
  CABIN DOOR
  CATWALK

10' 8"

STABILATOR TAB

STABILATOR

CATWALK
AILERON
FLAP
POSITION LIGHT (GREEN)

POSITION LIGHT (RED)
LANDING LIGHT
PITOT TUBE

𝕭eechcraft® MUSKETEER SUPER

MUSKETEER CUSTOM

53

Range: Includes warm-up, taxi, climb to altitude with 45-minute reserve. Reserve computed at 55% power.

75% power @ 7,000 feet .... 630 miles on 58.8 gallons
                                         385 miles on 38.8 gallons
                                         264 miles on 28.8 gallons

65% power @ 10,000 feet .... 759 miles on 58.8 gallons
                                        462 miles on 38.8 gallons
                                        314 miles on 28.8 gallons

55% power @ 10,000 feet .... 823 miles on 58.8 gallons
                                        501 miles on 38.8 gallons
                                        339 miles on 28.8 gallons

Weights

Gross weight utility category .... 2,200 pounds
Gross weight normal category .... 2,550 pounds
Empty weight (dry) .... 1,410 pounds
Useful load normal category .... 1,140 pounds

Useful load breakdown:
  Oil, fuel (28.8 gallons usable), 4 people, 265 lbs baggage
  Oil, fuel (38.8 gallons usable), 4 people, 205 lbs baggage
  Oil, fuel (58.8 gallons usable), 4 people, 85 lbs baggage

Baggage .... 270 pounds

Area

Wing .... 146.00 square feet

Dimensions

Wing span .... 32 feet, 9 inches
Length .... 25 feet, 0 inches
Height .... 8 feet, 3 inches
Cabin length (instrument panel aft) .... 95 inches
Cabin width .... 41 inches
Headroom (seat to ceiling)
  Front seat .... 39.25 inches
  Rear seat .... 37.75 inches
Baggage door size .... 18.5 by 23.75 inches
Cabin door size .... 38 by 40 inches

Technical Data:

Wing loading at gross weight (normal category) 17.47 pounds per square foot

Power loading at gross weight (normal category) 12.75 pounds per horsepower

Compartment volume:
  Baggage .... 19.5 cubic feet
  Hat shelf .... 3.8 cubic feet
Fuel capacity:
  Fuel 60 gallons .... 58.8 usable
  Oil 2 gallons .... 1.5 usable
Fuel specifications:
  Fuel .... 100/130 octane

Bonanza Comparison Tables

Model	Serial Number	Year
Model 35	D-1 to D-1500 inclusive	1947-1948
Model A35	D-1501 to D-2200 inclusive	1949
Model B35	D-2201 to D-2680 inclusive	1950
Model C35	D-2681 to D-3400 inclusive	1951-1952
Model D35	D-3401 to D-3698 inclusive	1953
Model E35	D-3699 to D-3998 inclusive	1954
Model F35	D-3999 to D-4391 inclusive	1955
Model G35	D-4392 to D-4865 inclusive	1956
Model H35	D-4866 to D-5330 inclusive	1957
Model J35	D-5331 to D-5725 inclusive	1958
Model K35	D-5726 to D-6161 inclusive	1959
Model M35	D-6162 to D-6561 inclusive	1960
Model N35	D-6562 to D-6841 inclusive	1961
Model P35	D-6842 to D-7309 inclusive	1962-1693
Model S35	D-7310 to D-7976 inclusive	1964-1965
Model V35	D-7977 to D-8598 inclusive	1966-1967
Model V35A	D-8599 to	1968-1969

Exceptions to the above are: D-3293, an E35 Model; D-4376, is a G35, and D-5062 is a J35.

Complete paint job began with the D35; extra rear windows with the F35; tinted windows with the D35; enlarged rear windows with the N35; fuel injection with the J35.

BEECHCRAFT BONANZA: 1947–1969 PRODUCTION MODELS

Year	Model	Price	Engine (Continental)	Weights			Speeds			Max. Range	Fuel	Rate of Climb
				Gross	Empty	Useful Load	Max.	Cruise	Stall			
1947	35	$ 8,945	E-185-1	2,550	1,458	1,092	184 mph	172 mph	55	750 st. mi.	39	950 fpm
1949	A35	$10,975	E-185-1	2,650	1,580	1,070	184 mph	170 mph	56	750 st. mi.	39	890 fpm
1950	B35	$11,975	E-185-8	2,650	1,575	1,075	184 mph	170 mph	56	750 st. mi.	39	890 fpm
1951	C35	$12,990	E-185-11	2,700	1,647	1,053	190 mph	175 mph	55	775 st. mi.	39	1,100 fpm
1953	D35	$18,990	E-185-11	2,725	1,650	1,075	190 mph	175 mph	55	775 st. mi.	39	1,100 fpm
1954	E35	$19,990	E-225-8	2,725	1,675	1,050	190 mph	175 mph	55	775 st. mi.	39	1,300 fpm
1955	F35	$19,990	E-225-8	2,750	1,697	1,053	194 mph	184 mph	55	775 st. mi.	39	1,300 fpm
1956	G35	$21,990	E-225-8	2,775	1,722	1,053	194 mph	184 mph	55	775 st. mi.	39	1,300 fpm
1957	H35	$22,650	O-470-G	2,900	1,833	1,067	206 mph	190 mph	55	775 st. mi.	39	1,300 fpm
1958	J35	$24,300	O-470-C	2,900	1,820	1,080	210 mph	200 mph	57	800 st. mi.	39	1,250 fpm
1959	K35	$25,300	IO-470-C	2,950	1,832	1,118	210 mph	200 mph	57	785 st. mi.	39	1,250 fpm
1960	M35	$25,300	IO-470-C	2,950	1,832	1,118	210 mph	195 mph	59	910 st. mi.	49	1,170 fpm
1961	N35	$26,500	IO-470-N	3,125	1,855	1,270	205 mph	195 mph	59	910 st. mi.	49	1,170 fpm
1962	P35	$26,825	IO-470-N	3,125	1,855	1,270	205 mph	195 mph	60	960 st. mi.	78	1,150 fpm
1964	S35	$28,750	IO-520-B	3,300	1,885	1,415	212 mph	205 mph	60	1,075 st. mi.	80	1,150 fpm
1966	V35	$31,425	IO-520-B	3,400	1,941	1,459	210 mph	203 mph	62	1,093 st. mi.	80	1,200 fpm
1966	V35TC	$37,750	TSIO-520-D	3,400	2,000	1,400	250 mph	230 mph	63	1,111 st. mi.	80	1,136 fpm
1967	V35A	$32,500	IO-520-B	3,400	1,935	1,465	210 mph	203 mph	63	1,082 st. mi.	80	1,225 fpm
1967	V35ATC	$37,750	TSIO-520-D	3,400	2,012	1,388	250 mph	230 mph	63	1,060 st. mi.	80	1,136 fpm
1968	E33	$30,750	IO-470-K	3,050	1,854	1,196	195 mph	185 mph	60	1,082 st. mi.	80	1,225 fpm
1968	E33A	$34,150	IO-520-B	3,300	1,900	1,400	208 mph	200 mph	61	1,170 st. mi.	80	930 fpm
1968	V35A	$35,750	IO-520-B	3,400	1,949	1,451	210 mph	203 mph	63	1,080 st. mi.	80	1,200 fpm
1968	V35A-TC	$40,950	TSIO-520-D	3,400	2,008	1,392	250 mph	230 mph	63	1,111 st. mi.	80	1,136 fpm
1969	E33	$31,750	IO-470-K	3,050	1,862	1,188	195 mph	185 mph	60	1,082 st. mi.	80	1,225 fpm
1969	E33A	$35,750	IO-520-B	3,300	1,915	1,385	208 mph	200 mph	61	1,170 st. mi.	80	930 fpm
1969	E33B	$34,250	IO-470-K	3,050	1,885	1,165	195 mph	185 mph	60	1,170 st. mi.	80	930 fpm

(2,800 aerobatic)

1969	E33C	$38,250	IO-520-B	3,300	1,918	1,382 (2,800 aerobatic)	208 mph	200 mph	61	1,080 st. mi.	80	1,200 fpm
1969	V35A	$36,850	IO-520-B	3,400	1,958	1,442	210 mph	203 mph	63	1,111 st. mi.	80	1,136 fpm
1969	V35A-TC	$42,750	TSIO-520-D	3,400	2,021	1,379	250 mph	230 mph	63	1,082 st. mi.	80	1,225 fpm
1969	36	$40,650	IO-520-B	3,600	1,980	1,620	204 mph	195 mph	64	980 st. mi.	80	1,015 fpm

Suggested selling price for 1966 and later includes standard avionics. Range includes fuel allowance for warm-up, taxi, take-off, and climb to altitude with 45 minute reserve at maximum range speed.

Original Bonanza Model 35 was powered with a Continental E-165-1 engine and had a top speed of 184 mph. It first flew December 22, 1945; received a Type Certificate in November, 1946. Deliveries began in March, 1947.

5. Bonanza! Earlier Models, including Debonairs

EARLY IN 1969, Mr. and Mrs. Lee D. Hagemeister, a Colorado couple and members of the International Flying Farmers, flew away from Wichita in their brand new Bonanza. It was the 9,000th Bonanza off the production lines in this model's 22-year history.

Now, since so many of these remain in service, and since so many are no longer in the hands of their original owners, perhaps it'll be useful if we'll go back a few years and relive demonstration flights we experienced in a Model P35 and Model S35 when each was brand-new. Then we'll return to the present and make a flight evaluation of a current model.

Let's start with the P35 Model on a January day in 1962. Here's the way we taped it that afternoon:

It's 1:40 PM; 30 degree F, with a five to seven mph southeast wind. Altimeter setting is 29.87 and the Kansas sky is a clear hard blue.

With us is Larry Ball, Beech's manager of Bonanza sales. Larry is a pleasant fellow, slender, a flyer all his adult life. He leads us across the ramp to N836H, a blue and white V-tail.

We trail along as Larry walks around the airplane for the pre-flight inspection. At the tail he explains that the control column moves both tail surfaces in the same direction, so that they act as elevators, while the rudder pedals operate these surfaces in opposite directions to act as rudders. Both controls may be operated simultaneously and the airplane will respond in the same manner as one with a conventional tail.

We continue around the plane and bend down to watch as Larry drains the fuel sediment bowl. We note the Bonanza's wide

Bonanza P35 was 1962/1963 model; engine was Continental IO-470-N of 260 hp. Top speed was 205 mph; best cruise, 195 mph.

track. "Sure like all that distance between the main gear wheels," we remark.

Larry nods. "Real easy to handle on the ground, and nice in a crosswind. It's strong, too. This gear was developed on the Beech T-34 Mentor to meet Navy specs for carrier landings. They demand a gear that can stand up under a twenty foot per second sink rate—equivalent to a free drop of fifteen feet."

We look impressed, and Larry points up at the wheel wells. "Notice that the main-wheel inboard doors are closed when the wheels are down. This keeps out mud and dirt and prevents buffeting damage in flight. And when the gear is up, everything is completely enclosed, clean as can be." He straightens up, completes his check, and we climb aboard.

He runs through the pretake-off check, then turns the key in the automobile-type ignition to awaken the 260 horses beneath the cowl.

The engine catches at once, and settles into the sewing-machine-like smoothness characteristic of this Continental fuel-injected powerplant—an engine that was originally designed especially for the Bonanza, we are told.

After taxiing to the runway and making the mag checks, Beech Tower consigns us to the Bonanza's natural habitat. Then Larry lifts her off at about 65 mph, and the electrically operated gear comes up with a whine.

We head for Newton, Kansas, and Larry demonstrates the P35's climb gaits. The steepest angle, handy for clearing obstacles from take-off, brings the air speed back to 80 mph. However, her best rate-of-climb seems to be at about 105 mph, with the vertical-speed indicator showing better than 1,300 feet per minute (we should mention here that we're loaded about 200 lbs under maximum allowable gross).

"In practice," Larry observes, "I usually settle for about a thousand feet per minute or slightly less. You can get that at a hundred and twenty-five or a hundred and thirty miles per hour and be in a much more comfortable attitude and with better visibility over the nose." He matches his words with the climb described. Then, lowering the nose a bit more, he ups air speed to 155 mph. The rate-of-climb hovers around 700 fpm; rpm's register 2,500, and the manifold pressure is at 25 inches of mercury.

Bonanza's wide track makes for easy ground handling and takes the work out of cross-wind landings and take-offs. Twin-engine Beechcraft Baron uses the same gear.

"How about flying straight and level for a few minutes," we ask, "to get a check on cruising speed at low altitude?"

He nods. "Okay. I'll drop back to two thousand feet and set power at seventy-five per cent." A minute later the air speed needle steadies at 176 mph indicated.

We time ourselves between some section lines below—the average of two runs in opposite directions—and the result is a ground speed of 180 mph. With altitude and temperature corrections fed

Bonanza's inboard landing gear doors are closed when gear is down to prevent buffeting damage in flight and keep out mud and dirt upon landing. Nose wheel has mud-scraper.

into our pocket computer, we get a true air speed of 184 mph—and this is at 2,000 ft. Clearly, the P35 Bonanza should have no trouble furnishing her factory-claimed 195 mph cruise at 7,000.

"Owners report all the time that they're getting a better cruise than we promise," Larry says contentedly. "We think that our advertised performance figures are conservative. It's better that way. No owner complaints—just bouquets." He's quiet a minute, then adds, "Of course, it's possible to mount a lot of aerials and stuff on the outside and markedly cut into your speed."

"Why don't we check her stall characteristics?" we ask.

"Okay. What kind of stalls do you want?"

"How about stalling her out of a turn? You know, like turning on final approach without power."

He nods agreement. "Let's go up a little higher."

A few minutes later we level off at 6,000 feet. Larry eases back on the throttle, drops the landing gear, and 30 degrees of flap. Then, as the air speed unwinds below 90 mph, we roll into a 30-degree left turn. He grins at us. "Remember, we're making this landing pattern at six thousand feet."

We shrug unsympathetically. Beauty is as beauty does, we're thinking. No matter how well she's built, or how pretty she is, if she's got some bad habits it's our job to try and find them. We watch the air speed needle fall behind 70 mph. The nose is high. The pay-off is close.

Then things begin to happen. The stall warning horn blows, and the aft section of the fuselage begins an airborne version of the twist. This goes on for several seconds—plenty of warning time —and she's doing everything but kick our shins to let us know how we're mistreating her.

She breaks from the stall rather sharply—as you would expect in such a clean aircraft—but the important thing is that she breaks straight ahead and the left wing comes up smoothly.

Larry grins at us again. "The defense rests," he says.

"All right. Suppose we try some short landings and take-offs." Our friend does not mention it, but we note that the stall recovery required but 100 feet of altitude.

"Since we're this high," Larry says, "we're afforded a good opportunity to check the P35's rapid descent ability." He comes back on the throttle, raises flaps (but leaves the landing gear down), then shoves the control column toward the instrument panel.

We nose-down at an extremely steep angle, and our instincts urge us to do two things immediately: get that control wheel back where it belongs, and take a look at the air speed indicator. We can't do anything about the control wheel; so we cast an apprehensive eye at the air speed. It's holding steady at 150 mph. The

Bonanza wing test, simulating aileron roll. Top load of 2,700 lbs. simulates air load; bottom loads, of 280 lbs. each, simulate aileron loads applied through aileron hinge brackets.

rate-of-climb indicator shows a 3,000 fpm let-down—which our ears painfully confirm—but there's no speed build-up.

Then, still making like a dive bomber, Larry drops the flaps and the air speed falls back to 120 mph; rate of descent remains at 3,000 fpm.

We level off again and run through a few more stalls; one "clean," one "dirty." With power off, wheels and flaps up, the nose drops out from under us at an indicated 65 mph. With gear and flaps down, the stall comes at a fraction under 60. Each time considerable tail buffeting follows the mechanical stall-warning system in the cabin. To our way of thinking, planes that shake their tails like the V-tailed Bonanzas (most of this is lost in the conventional-tailed Bonanzas) have the best stall-warning devices ever made. It's impossible to ignore, comes in plenty of time for corrective action, and unlike mechanical gadgets, it can never fail.

Each time we stalled this airplane, she broke straight ahead, and each time the wings were level or nearly so.

Minimum Field. We continue earthward and, a few minutes later, enter the traffic pattern at Newton. We fly the pattern at 120 mph, and, although Larry explains that normally the final should be made with an over-the-fence speed of 80, this time he drops down very low on a long final—and very slow.

Lined-up with the runway, we are about 300 yards from the fence. With gear and flaps down, and the P35 in landing configuration (nose high) only a few feet above the ground, we creep in under minimum power with an indicated air speed of 60 mph! Ordinarily, this caper would bother us considerably; but aware of the V-tail's stall habits we sit back unconcerned, secure in the knowledge that, as long as she doesn't shake her tail like a wet dog, we're fat.

Over the fence then, and, just as the edge of the concrete slides beneath the nose, Larry chops power and 36H squats solidly. We're sure that the main gear touched within the first ten feet of the runway.

Our friend stands on the brakes. The tires squeal but don't skid. Forgotten camera equipment in back slams against our seats. The plane stops. "Want to measure it?" Larry inquires.

We nod and jump out to mark the spot then Larry taxis off the runway.

A couple of minutes later we return to the airplane with teeth chattering and grateful for the Bonanza's high-output cabin heater. "Three hundred and fifty-seven feet," we announce.

He frowns. "Cool as it is, she should do better than that. Let's try again."

It seems pretty good to us, but he's so obviously disturbed about it that we acquiesce. "Okay. Let's see how short you can get her off." (Measuring the landing, we discovered that the expansion joints in Newton's runway are 21 feet apart. We'll count these as they sail by on take-off).

Larry swings back to the end of the strip, sets brakes, adds flaps and opens the throttle. With maximum power going for us, he turns her loose and, it seems to us from the corner of our eye (we're counting expansion joints), that he comes back on the wheel within ten or eleven seconds.

Twelve, thirteen, fourteen—the last few joints really fly by. We stop counting at sixteen as the P35 claws heavenward. "Three hundred and thirty-six feet," we say.

He nods, apparently satisfied.

We're back a few minutes later, and again we tip-toe up to the runway, nose-high and holding minimum power. This time we have 58 mph indicated. We touch down within spitting distance of the runway's beginning, and again the tires protest loudly. Again we measure.

"Three hundred and thirty feet this time, Larry!"

His grin returns. "Guess that's about as good as we'll do without an arresting hook."

We agree. According to the P35 owner's manual, this aircraft normally requires a landing roll of 505 feet. Normal take-off is given as 745 feet. Perhaps we should add that the wind was nearly straight down the runway at 7 mph. Newton is 1,480 feet above sea level; ground temperture was 30 degrees F., barometric pressure was 29.85—and we were almost 200 lbs below gross.

Modified Tail. Some years ago, when the early Bonanzas began flying, there was some talk concerning this plane's proclivity to "hunt" in rough air—to swing her nose a bit from side to side. This tendency (and it was more of a tendency than a full-blown trait) was corrected beginning with the Model C35 when the tail surfaces were enlarged and given a slightly greater dihedral angle. On the way back to Beech from Newton, we stooged around in light turbulence for ten or fifteen minutes, and we could detect no indication of the P35's wingtips racing one another. She rode the gentler swells gracefully; occasionally took a sharp punch on a wing. Several times we had to rudder her back on course after an uneven buffeting; but in our judgment she revealed no trace of vice. The P35 is as honest as a Kansas sunrise.

P35 SPECIFICATIONS AND PERFORMANCE

Engine: Continental 6-cyl. IO-470N, rated at 260 hp @ 2625 rpm.

Wing area & loadings
Wing area .... 181 sq. ft.
Wing loading at gross weight .... 17.27 lb./sq. ft.
Power loading at gross weight .... 12.02 lb./hp.

Weights
Maximum gross, std. model .... 3,125 lbs.
Maximum gross, optional 5-place .... 3,125 lbs.
Empty weight, std. model .... 1,855 lbs.
Empty weight, optional 5-place .... 1,872 lbs.
Useful load (fuel, oil, optional equipment, passengers
and baggage) .... 1,270 lbs.
Available weight for people, baggage and optional equip-
ment with standard tanks full .... 948 lbs.

Baggage
Volume .... 16.5 cu. ft.
Including utility shelf .... 22.4 cu. ft.
Capacity (5th seat unoccupied) .... 270 lbs.

Fuel & oil capacity
Fuel, std. tanks (25 gal. each wing) .... 49 gal. usable.
Fuel, long-range tanks (39 gal. each wing) .... 78 gal. usable.
Oil capacity .... 10 qts.

Dimensions
Wing span .... 33 ft. 5½ in.
Length .... 25 ft. 2 in.
Height .... 6 ft. 6½ in.

Cabin dimensions
Cabin length, upper .... 8 ft. 6 in.
Cabin length, lower .... 6 ft. 11 in.
(Cabin lengths measured from instrument panel aft).
Cabin width .... 3 ft. 6 in.
Cabin height .... 4 ft. 2 in.
Passenger door size .... 36 in × 37 in.

Baggage door size .... 18½ in × 22½ in.
Glass area .... 26 sq. ft.

P35 PERFORMANCE

Cruising speeds

75% power (2450 rpm) at 7,000 ft .... 195 mph.
65% power (2450 rpm) at 10,000 ft .... 190 mph.
45% power (2300 rpm) at 10,000 ft .... 159 mph.
High speed at sea level (2625 rpm) .... 205 mph.

Range: (These figures include full allowance for warm-up, taxi, take-off and climb to altitude with 45-minute reserve at maximum-range speed.)

45% power at 10,000 ft., w/std. tanks .... 690 mi.
45% power at 10,000 ft., w/long-range tanks .... 1,215 mi.
65% power at 10,000 ft., w/std. tanks .... 610 mi.
65% power at 10,000 ft., w/long-range tanks .... 1,075 mi.
75% power at 7,000 ft., w/std. tanks .... 540 mi.
75% power at 7,000 ft., w/long-range tanks .... 960 mi.

Rate of climb at sea level .... 1,150 fpm
Service ceiling .... 19,200 ft.
Absolute ceiling .... 21,000 ft.

Stall speeds

Gear and flaps down, power off .... 60 mph.
Gear and flaps up, power off .... 71 mph.

Take-off distance

Std. atmosphere, 10 mph wind, 20-deg. flap .... 745 ft.
Over 50-ft. obstacle .... 1,050 ft.

Take-off speeds

Normal .... 65 mph/56.5 kts.
Climb-out at 50 ft. .... 80 mph/69.5 kts.
Minimum run take-off .... 60 mph/52.1 kts.
Minimum run & climb-out at 50 ft. .... 80 mph/69.5 kts.
Obstacle .... 60 mph/52.1 kts.
Cimb-out after obstacle take-off .... 65 mph/56.5 kts.

Landing distance

Std. atmosphere, 10 mph wind, 30-deg. flap .... 505 ft.
Total over 50-ft. obstacle .... 840 ft.

Landing speeds

Normal approach speed .... 78 mph/67.6 kts.
Normal contact speed .... 65 mph/56.5 kts.
Obstacle approach speed .... 72 mph/62.5 kts.
Obstacle contact speed .... 65 mph/56.5 kts.

Note: all figures based on maximum gross weight.

We Fly the S35 Bonanza. Our check-flight in the new S35 Bonanza in 1964 almost threatened to be more than we had bargained for. Actually, the flight itself was a pleasurable one; it was the anticipation that caused us to skip our breakfast.

It all began the night before when we were having dinner with Champion Aerobatic Pilot, Harold Krier, and we casually mentioned that we were scheduled to fly the new S35 at the Beech factory next morning. Harold, who is a very quiet-voiced and modest-type aviator, replied that he'd heard some nice things about this plane and would like to try it out himself. Naturally, we insisted that he come along.

Back at the motel alone, however, we began to have second thoughts. What did he mean by the term "like to try it out?" Did he intend to do a cobra-roll or two? Maybe a few hammerhead stalls and some inverted Cuban-eights? After all, we'd watched Hal perform professionally many times and knew he usually began his heart-stopping exhibitions by rolling inverted on take-off about 20 feet above the runway, then climbing-out upside down. But surely he wouldn't—still, you could never tell. . . .

Next morning at eight, we met Larry Ball on the flight line and Larry introduced us to N7917K. It was red and white with a black detail stripe—exactly the same color as Harold's famed KrierKraft (this was just before Hal switched to his Chipmunk).

We were downright apprehensive by the time Harold arrived, and he was altogether too cheerful and alert, we thought, as he said something about not having had time to eat breakfast.

"Who needs it?" we mumbled inaudibly.

We took off with Harold handling the controls from the left-hand seat. It was a very conventional take-off, with a left turn out of the pattern at 500 feet. We looked at Harold suspiciously and took a firm grip on pencil, pad, and tape recorder.

With full tanks, three of us aboard, but without luggage, One-Seven-Kilo was still a bit under maximum gross weight, and rate-of-climb indicated 1,400 fpm. Temperature had read 80 degrees F on the ground, with an altimeter setting of 29.92. There was a broken cumulus overcast at 3,000 feet, and our aerobatic friend picked a hole and scooted through.

True Air Speeds. We continued upward to 6,500; trimmed, and noted 185 mph indicated. This with an outside air temp of 62 degrees F and at 75% power. At 65% power (2,300 rpms), we had 180 indicated at this altitude. Harold then cut her back to 45% power (1,850 rpms), and this resulted in the fuel-flow meter

69

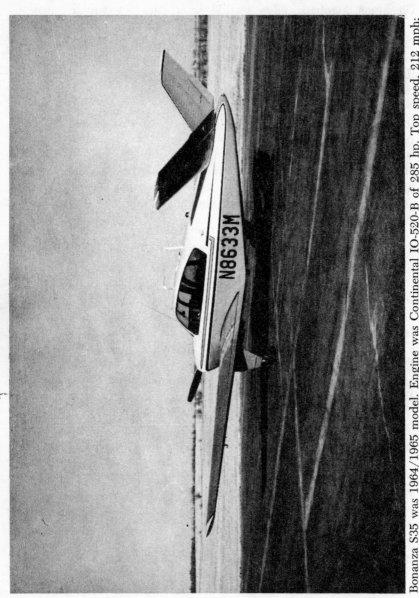

Bonanza S35 was 1964/1965 model. Engine was Continental IO-520-B of 285 hp. Top speed, 212 mph; cruise, 205 mph. Fuselage pointy tail was new.

dropping to 9.9 gallons per hour at an indicated air speed of 158 mph.

We then carefully lined up temp with pressure altitude in the window of our E-6B computer and transposed the above indicated air speeds to true air speeds of 209 mph, 203 mph and 178 mph respectively. Now Beech claims but 205 mph with 75% power at 6,500 for the 285 hp S35 pointy-tail, so it would appear that Larry's claim concerning the conservatism of Beech's advertised performance figures is a valid one.

In the stall department, the S35 quit flying for Harold at about 70 mph indicated, power off and clean. Like her earlier sister models, she shakes her tail very stubbornly several seconds before the pay-off.

And yes, fans, she does do beautiful chandelles—and at 200 mph (yes, we know all about "maximum maneuvering speed;" we're merely reporting what happened). At this speed, the G-load is somewhat more than we are used to, but under the hand of this master chandelle-maker it is a smooth maneuver and an exhilarating one. But Harold relented before we turned green, and went down to Newton Municipal for a check on this plane's short-field capability.

But by this time, it was 90 degrees F on the ground and very bumpy below cloud height. We tried several approaches and maximum-performance take-offs, but under the conditions were unable to better the performance of the P35 Model—which, admittedly, we had done on a cold day and in smooth air. In this connection, Larry did mention that the built-in drag accruing to the S35 equipped with optional three-bladed prop gave that plane markedly shorter landings.

Since there was no cafe at Newton Municipal, and since Hal had mildly reminded us that he'd had no breakfast, we decided to go to Hutchinsen Municipal and take advantage of the excellent cafeteria in the terminal building there. On the way, we went to 8,000 feet this time to find smooth air (the cumulus were beginning to take on vertical build-up), and also to allow Hal to check the S35's climb gaits. As expected, the S35 is a bit superior to the P35 in all climb attitudes. We reached 8,000 in 7 minutes, 22 seconds from lift-off at Newton.

S35 "Sailplane." "Suppose we could glide from here into Hutchinsen?" Harold asked no one in particular.

"We could come pretty close," Larry said. "We're about twenty miles away, and the book says the S-Model will glide fifteen miles from this altitude with a full load."

Krier cut the throttle and put the prop in low rpm.

"Hold her at about 90 mph," Larry advised, "and turn off the electrical system to keep the landing-gear warning horn quiet."

Harold tidied up the panel as directed and adjusted the air speed with the control wheel. He grinned. "Some sailplane!"

We noted that the vertical-speed indicator recorded a rate-of-descent of 800 feet per minute; but Harold gained back about 50 fpm of this with careful trim. It was whisper-quiet. The nose seemed almost level; and with no physical sensation of sinking it felt as if we could float endlessly. But Harold was hungry; so, at 6,000 feet, he fed in power again and we raced downhill into Hutchinsen with the air speed needle crowding the red line. His only comment was: "She sure likes to go, doesn't she?"

Over breakfast, Larry mentioned some features of the S35 that we may have overlooked: cabin 19 inches longer; increased baggage area; new cabin heating system with 30% increase in heat output; 145 lbs additional payload, and a gear-driven alternator which gives 20 amps electrical power at idle and 70 amps at only 1,700 rpms. There was more medium-hard sell from Beech's manager of Bonanza sales, but at that point we shut down our end of the operation to attack our bacon and eggs. We hadn't had any breakfast either.

S35 SPECIFICATIONS AND PERFORMANCE

Engine: Continental 6-cyl. IO-520B, rated at 285 hp @ 2,700 rpm.

Weights

Gross	3,300 lbs.
Empty	1,885 lbs.
Useful load	1,415 lbs.
Available for people, baggage, optional equipment, with standard tanks full	1,089 lbs.
Maximum baggage	270 lbs.

Dimensions

Wing span	33 ft. 5½ in.
Length	26 ft. 4⅝ in.
Height (tail section)	7 ft. 7 in.

Cabin dimensions
Cabin length (instrument panel aft) .... 8 ft. 6 in.
Cabin width .... 3 ft. 6 in.
Cabin height .... 4 ft. 2 in.
Passenger door size .... 36 in. × 27 in.
Baggage door size .... 22½ in. × 18½ in.
Baggage compartment volume .... 33½ cu. ft.

Cruising speeds
75% power (2500 rpm) at 6,500 ft. .... 205 mph/178 kts.
65% power (2500 rpm) at 10,000 ft. .... 200 mph/174 kts.
55% power (2300 rpm) at 10,000 ft. .... 186 mph/162 kts.
100% power (2700 rpm) at sea level .... 212 mph/184 kts.

Range: (including warm-up, taxi, take-off, climb to altitude and 45 minutes of reserve fuel)
55% power at 10,000 ft. .... 592 mi./49 gal.
55% power at 10,000 ft. .... 1,093 mi./80 gal.
65% power at 10,000 ft. .... 552 mi./49 gal.
65% power at 10,000 ft. .... 1,016 mi./80 gal.
75% power at 6,500 ft. .... 510 mi./49 gal.
75% power at 6,500 ft. .... 925 mi./80 gal.
Rate of climb at sea level .... 1,200 fpm.
Service ceiling .... 18,300 ft.
Absolute ceiling .... 20,000 ft.

Stall speeds, power off
Gear and flaps down 30 degrees .... 62 mph.
Gear and flaps up .... 73 mph.

Take-off distance (20-deg. flap, sea level, 59 deg. F)
Ground run .... 880 ft.
Total over 50-ft. obstacle .... 1,225 ft.

Landing distance (30-deg. flap, sea level, 59 deg. F)
Ground roll .... 625 ft.
Total over 50-ft. obstacle .... 1,150 ft.

Note: all figures based on maximum gross weight.

Debonair-Bonanza B33. The Beechcraft Debonair is, and always has been, a Bonanza with a conventional tail. Except for the extra feather in its tail, the Debonair airframe is the Bonanza airframe. Finally, in 1968, Beech dropped the name "Debonair" and faced up to reality. The former Debonair was renamed Bonanza Model E33. So, let's go back one more time to take a demonstration ride in a 1963 Debonair/Bonanza Model B33.

It's a brilliant spring day, with a few scattered cloud-sheep grazing on warm thermals at 8,000 feet. On the ground, it's 57 degrees F; wind is west-southwest at 13 mph and the barometer is steady at 30.13 inches.

We walk around the new B33 while Larry simultaneously gives it a preflight check and us a sales talk. This craft is painted tan-and-white and trimmed in red. Her registration is N1513S—One-Three-Sugar—and this is, according to Larry, a very appropriate designation. "An airplane as sweet as the B33," he says shamelessly, "deserves to be called 'sugar!'"

We nod absently while watching a pilot nearby fruitlessly grind the starter of a Cessna 210. "What do you suppose is wrong with that Brand X airplane?" we ask.

"I'll give you eight-to-five there's nothing wrong with the airplane," Larry replies. "It's just that that fellow hasn't bothered to read his owner's manual. Doubt if he could start this one while it's hot either."

"Meaning?"

"He's been flying carburetor-equipped airplanes and is just switching over to a fuel-injected engine. All he's got to do is read the directions on the label. The main thing he must understand is that his auxiliary fuel pump acts as a *primer* while cranking his engine. Once this is understood, he'll find that he has the easiest-starting engine he's ever flown."

The other pilot has left his plane and is heading for the hangar so we climb aboard the B33 as Larry mentions that its 225 hp fuel-injected Continental burns 80 octane gasoline if we happen to be economy-minded.

While taxiing to the runway, we determine that One-Three-Sugar is about 400 pounds under maximum gross weight with only two of us aboard and a lightly loaded baggage compartment. Larry sets altimeter at field elevation, 1,108 feet. Then, after mag check and exercising the prop, we roll onto the runway and accelerate for take-off.

About 400 feet downfield a photographer is waiting to get a shot of us as we become airborne—but Sugar wants to fly. When we flash past the photographer we are 50 feet in the air. At 57 degrees F and 400 lbs light, Sugar is downright impatient.

We remain in the traffic pattern and return to our take-off point. We come over the fence at 80 mph crabbing into the wind at an angle of about 15 degrees from the centerline of the N-S runway. She sticks-on very nicely and we squeal to a stop a good 50 feet before reaching our cameraman.

We listen to the photographer's complaint that we are not cooperating, and suggest that he move a bit closer to our starting point.

We taxi back to the end of the runway, set brakes, add flap, and feed in full power. We release the brakes and the B33 leaps forward. We pick up speed very quickly, but then we see that our photographer friend has moved much closer than we'd intended. He's crouched on the edge of the runway less than 300 feet from our starting point.

Sugar tries hard, but we're asking too much. Her elevators lift her off, but then we settle back and she roars on a few more feet at a reduced angle-of-attack before her wings will support us. And Larry's criticism is a masterpiece of tact: "The B33's elevator control is very good," he says. "As you just saw, firm back-pressure on the wheel will lift you a few feet into the air before the airplane is actually ready to fly."

Within seconds after lift-off, the rate-of-climb indicator is bouncing against the 1,800 fpm mark. Indicated air speed is 100 to 103 mph, and Larry observes that the abnormal climb rate is due to our light loading. "That's quite a bit better than the plane will do fully loaded, especially on a hotter day."

We put Sugar on the step at 3,000 feet with 75% power. It's bumpy here; we're well below cloud height and boring through a bunch of thermals. The air speed needle bounces between 166 and 176 mph. We watch it for quite a while, but it doesn't want to steady down. We finally decide to call it 172 mph. Then, using the "add 2% per thousand feet" rule, we get a true air speed of about 182 mph at this altitude.

Then we go to 7,000 feet, which is where, all things considered, the B33 should perform most efficiently. We are still below the cumulus patches, which are feeding upon the tall thermals, but we seem to have found a section of sky where they are less numerous. It's smoother here. Again, we trim carefully, and set the plane at her minimum angle-of-attack. Manifold pressure is 22 inches; rpms: 2,450. We make sure that the altimeter and rate-of-climb are steady, then watch the air speed needle. It points proudly at 167 mph. Again employing the old "2% per thousand feet" rule, we come up with a true air speed of 190 mph. But as a double check we run it through our pocket computer—noting outside air temp of 25 degrees at this altitude—and confirm that we're doing a fraction over 190 mph. That's a five mph bonus over Beech's advertised figure.

B33 Stalls. "How about some stalls, Larry?"

He grins. "Go ahead. I know you've got that hang-up about trying stalls out of turns. Be my guest."

We slow the plane and, as the air speed drops below 165 mph, we lower the landing gear. (Maximum gear-down speed for the B33—and V-tails, too, prior to 1968—is 165 mph. However, in an emergency, the gear may be lowered up to 200 mph, although it may result in some damage to the gear doors.) With gear and flap lowered, and with the left wing cocked down at a 30-degree angle, the stall comes at about 58 mph indicated. The break is sharp, although the wing comes up instantly and we plunge straight ahead with good aileron control.

Compared with the V-tail, the B33's stall behavior is much the same as that of its sister. However, there is one big difference: the B33 lacks the pronounced tail-buffeting displayed by the V-tail models just before stall. In the B33 you have, in addition to the air speed indicator staring at you, only a moderate tremble in the control wheel on the edge of stall—plus the mechanical stall-warning horn. With the horn's sensor vane properly set, the horn begins a tentative, intermittent beeping several miles per hour and six or seven seconds ahead of full stall (we're not speaking of an extremely abrupt maneuver, of course). During the last five seconds—which is, clearly, plenty of time for correction—the horn sounds steadily and insistently.

This is purely a personal thing; but, especially low and slow, we do feel a lot more comfortable with the V-tail's aerodynamic stall-warning "device."

Next, we try some stalls from level flight. With gear and flaps down, power off, the break comes at about 56 mph (remember, we're 400 lbs light. Fully loaded, the advertised figure of 60 should be about right). With gear and flaps up and power off, full stall is reached at 68 mph indicated as nearly as we can tell—we're bouncing in mild turbulence again.

Then, recalling Larry's demonstration of the P35's rapid-descent ability, we ask if the B33 is capable of matching it.

He motions for the wheel. We swing it over to him. He cuts throttle, drops landing gear and shoves the wheel forward. A few seconds later, the rate-of-descent is registered at 3,500 fpm. Air speed is steady at 165 mph indicated. With flaps added, air speed falls back to 130–135 mph, while rate-of-descent slows to 3,000 fpm.

Returning to the airport we have time to reflect that the B33 has a lighter feel than its V-tailed sister; it responds a little quicker. This is an advantage or disadvantage depending upon personal preference. Personally, we like the way the V-tail seems to sometimes smooth-out our not-always-precise coordination. But the B33 leaves the impression that she likes to be *flown,* and is eager to react to anything one asks of her. However, trimmed for cruise in level flight, the B33, like the V-tail, is very stable and seems content to sit there all day and eat up the miles with a minimum of attention from the pilot.

Speaking of stability, Larry tells us that the Bonanza/Debonairs offer the non-instrument flyer an unusual safety feature if he's ever caught above an overcast and has to land. All he has to do is: 1) slow down to 100 mph and lower the gear; 2) keep hands off the control wheel and adjust trim for a 500 fpm let-down at 100 mph, and 3) use rudder pedals alone to hold an approximate desired heading. According to Larry, time, God, and a good airplane will take care of the details.

B33 SPECIFICATIONS AND PERFORMANCE

Engine: Continental 6-cyl. IO-470K, rated at 225 hp @ 2600 rpm.

Weights

Gross weight	3,000 lbs.
Empty weight	1,745 lbs.
Useful load	1,255 lbs.
Available for people, baggage, and optional equipment with standard tanks full	933 lbs.

Wing area & loadings

Wing area	177.6 sq. ft.
Wing loading at gross weight	16.9 lbs./sq. ft.
Power loading at gross weight	13.3 lbs./hp.

Baggage

Volume	16.5 cu. ft.
Capacity	270 lbs.

Dimensions

Wing span	32 ft. 10 in.

```
Length ............................................... 25 ft.  6 in.
Height ............................................... 8 ft.  3 in.
Cabin length ......................................... 6 ft. 11 in.
Cabin width .......................................... 3 ft. 6 in.
Cabin height ......................................... 4 ft. 2 in.
Passenger door size ................................. 36 in. × 37 in.
Baggage door size .................................. 20 in. × 24 in.
```

Fuel & oil capacity
```
Fuel, standard tanks (25 gal. each) ................... 49 gal. usable
Fuel, long range tanks (39.75 gal. each) .............. 78 gal. usable.
Oil .................................................... 10 qts.
```

Cruising speeds
```
75% power (2450 rpm) at  7,000 ft. ...................... 185 mph
65% power (2450 rpm) at 11,000 ft. ...................... 180 mph
50% power (2100 rpm) at 10,000 ft. ...................... 154 mph
Top Speed (2600 rpm) at sea level ...................... 195 mph
```

Range: (Includes full allowance for fuel used during warm-up, taxiing, take-off, and climb to altitude plus a 45-minute reserve at maximum speed)
```
50% power at 10,000 ft., std. fuel tanks ...................   645 mi.
50% power at 10,000 ft., long-range tanks ................. 1,135 mi.
65% power at 11,000 ft., std. fuel tanks ...................   595 mi.
65% power at 11,000 ft., long-range tanks ................. 1,050 mi.
75% power at  7,000 ft., std. fuel tanks ...................   540 mi.
75% power at  7,000 ft., long-range tanks .................   940 mi.
```

Rate of climb at sea level .... 960 fpm.

Service ceiling .... 18,400 ft.

Absolute ceiling .... 20,500 ft.

Stall speeds, power off
```
Gear down and 30 degrees flap ........................... 60 mph
Gear and flaps up ....................................... 71 mph
```

Take-off distance (20 degrees flaps)
```
Ground run (sea level, no wind, 59 deg. F) ................... 940 ft.
```

C33 AND C33A SPECIFICATIONS AND PERFORMANCES

	C33	C33A
Engine	Continental 6-cyl. IO-470K, rated at 225 hp @ 2600 rpm.	Continental 6-cyl. IO-520B, rated at 285 hp @ 2700 rpm.
Weights		
Gross weight	3050 lbs.	3300 lbs.
Useful load	1270 lbs.	1400 lbs.
Dimensions		
Wing span	32 ft. 10 in.	same
Length	25 ft. 6 in.	same
Height	8 ft. 3 in.	same

Wing area & loadings		
Wing area	177.6 sq. ft.	same
Wing loading (at gross weight)	17.2 lbs./sq. ft.	18.58 lbs./sq. ft.
Power loading (at gross weight)	13.5 lbs./hp	11.58 lbs./hp
Cabin dimensions		
Length	6 ft 11 in.	same
Width	3 ft. 6 in.	same
Height	4 ft. 2 in.	same
Fuel & oil capacity		
Fuel (std. tanks)	50 gal.	same
Fuel (long-range)	80 gal.	same
Oil	10 qts.	12 qts.
Speeds		
Cruise @ 75% power at 7,000 feet	185 mph	202 mph
Top speed, sea level	194 mph	209 mph
Cruising range		
At 65% power at 10,000 ft.	595 mi. (std. fuel)	539 mi. (std. fuel)
	1075 mi. (opt. fuel)	989 mi. (opt. fuel)
At 75% power at 7,000 ft.	540 mi. (std. fuel)	495 mi. (std. fuel)
	965 mi. (opt. fuel)	896 mi. (opt fuel)
Rate of climb (sea level)	930 fpm	1,136 fpm
Service ceiling	17,800 ft.	17,500 ft.
Absolute ceiling	20,000 ft.	20,000 ft.
Stall power off		
Gear & flaps 30 deg.	60 mph	62 mph
Gear & flaps up	71 mph	73 mph
Take-off distance, 20 deg. flaps		
Ground run	982 ft.	950 ft.
Over 50-ft. obstacle	1,298 ft.	1,177 ft.
Landing distance		
Ground run	643 ft.	647 ft.
Over 50-ft. obstacle	1,298 ft.	1,177 ft.

6. Bonanza! V35A, E33, Model 36, V35A-TC

THE ORIGIN OF the Bonanza can be traced back to the thirties when Walter Beech directed that preliminary design studies begin on an eventual successor to the Staggerwing. At that time, Beech and his engineers investigated the butterfly tail proposed by Georges Rudlicki.

Rudlicki, an aircraft designer working for E. P. T. Laskiewicz, a Lublin, Poland, airframe builder, conceived the V-tail along with other configurations such as an inverted V, a W and an M, and tested them in wind tunnels as well as on actual aircraft.

The Polish designer settled upon the V-tail because it weighed 35% less than a conventional tail, reduced drag and therefore increased speed, and because in military applications of that time

Bonanza V35A of 1968–1969 is fitted with Continental IO-520-B of 285 hp. Top speed 210 mph; cruise, 203 mph. Higher gross weight and useful load, plus new cabin ventilation system, cost two mph in speed.

it would afford rear gunners better visibility and increased field of fire to the rear.

Beech Aircraft's research and development program on the V-tail covered a number of years and it was exhaustively flown during the early forties installed on an AT-10, a twin-engined Beechcraft that served as a transitional trainer for the Army Air Forces in WW II.

A vast amount of essential engineering data was obtained from the V-tail AT-10 experiments, information that was vital in development of the Bonanza, but that was only one phase of Beech's project to introduce a revolutionary lightplane following the war.

Another important consideration was the Bonanza's wing. In the end, the choice was narrowed to two principal types of wing configurations. Both were subjected to rigorous test and evaluation. One was a laminar flow section, the other a version of the NACA 23000 Series, which was eventually adopted.

Also, before the Bonanza prototype was flown, a far-reaching ground test program was conducted. Structural components were assaulted with the equivalent of 20,000 flying hours of stress.

Finally, on December 22, 1945, veteran Beech test pilot Vern Carstens took the prototype Bonanza into the air for the first time. An intensive flight-test program stretched through 1946, and Bonanza Model 35 production began following type certification in November, 1946.

The performance and utility of the Bonanza led Beech to development of the Model 45 Mentor, a military training plane that has long served the Air Force, Navy and many friendly nations. The tandem-seat, two-place Mentor was derived from the basic Bonanza airframe, and, in appreciation, gave back to the Bonanza the Mentor's rugged landing gear.

Accuracy of engineering projections relating to the growth potential of the original Bonanza design has been solidly proven through the years. Without any major redesign, the Bonanza powerplant has evolved from the first 165 hp unit of the Model 35 to the present 225 and 285 hp engines. During this time, gross weight of the Bonanza has increased from 2,500 pounds to the 3,600 pounds of the six-place Bonanza 36.

Speaking of redesign, two airframe improvements were made in the Bonanza which, though Beech does not regard them as "major," have certainly made a major difference: one was larger tail surfaces with increased dihedral angle beginning with the C35 Model, and the other was an improved wing structure beginning with the F35 Model.

The structural integrity of the Bonanza is such that the Bonanza/Debonair Series constitute the only high-performance, single-engine business airplanes licensed by the FAA for Utility Category use at full gross weight. A Utility Category aircraft must safely withstand 4.4 times its design gross weight in specific flying conditions, while aircraft licensed in the Normal Category require only 3.8 load limit factor.

Late in 1965, Beech Aircraft announced the V35 Model and the

All Bonanza interiors are luxurious. Note excellent rearward visibility.
Bonanzas have 27 sq. ft. of glass area in late models.

new turbocharged V35TC. Exterior changes (in addition to a new paint job) were a one-piece windshield and a fresh air scoop mounted just forward of the V-tail. Inside, instrumentation was improved by addition of a turn coordinator as standard equipment, and a new flap-position indicator that shows flap position by degrees on the panel. Interior air inlets were also enlarged and repositioned, while the aft-mounted outside air inlet further cut the noise-level inside an already relatively quiet cabin.

By 1969, Beech had seven models in the Bonanza line, counting the Model 33, formerly known as the Debonair. These included the V35A V-tail, the conventional-tailed Model 33 in four versions (the 285 hp E33A, 225 hp E33, and aerobatic versions of each), the turbocharged V35A-TC V-tail, and the stretched "station wagon" Bonanza Model 36 which has a conventional tail.

We went to Wichita to fly the V35A and were introduced to it by Beech's Larry Long on a hot July morning. It was already 84 degrees F on the ground at 8:30 AM; it would be one of those brassy-hot days on the plains with vagrant convection winds born of thermal activity as the sun rose higher. Barometric pressure: 30.01 (Beech Field is 1,387 feet above sea level), and Beech Tower reported wind as NW at five mph.

Larry Long is a big man—"Two hundred and fifteen pounds with shaving cream on." We add our own 160 pounds, plus full tanks (50 gallons) and 40 lbs of cameras and other paraphernalia including our tape recorder, and the total is 715 lbs. This leaves us 427 lbs below gross. (Complete specs and performance tables for the V35A are at the end of this chapter.)

Preflighting the Bonanza, we notice a backwards-facing air scoop on the port side of the fuselage at the rear of the cabin. Larry explains that this little opening acts as a venturi tube to draw air from the cabin in flight and provide a gentle but positive circulation, while increasing heating and cooling efficiency.

Taxiing to the south end of Beech Field, Larry points out that the gyros are pressure-driven and backed-up with electrical drive. If one system should fail, you still have your gyro-controlled flight instruments. The B-5 Auto Pilot, a two-axis device with altitude hold, is married to the turn coordinator.

"Frankly, we did have a few complaints concerning the altitude-hold function on earlier auto pilots," Larry says, "but that's been

Bonanzas are licensed in the Utility Category, which means their airframes must be 15% stronger than civil aircraft licensed for normal operation. This is fuselage interior looking aft.

corrected. I've flown this one on long cross-country flights many times now, and it always maintains altitude within twenty feet of the number I select."

On the run-up pad at the south end of Beech Field (just off Kellog Avenue), we check the prop at 1,900 rpms, the mags at 1,700 rpms, then confirm that door and windows are closed. Beech Tower gives us the nod and we swing onto the runway.

"Lighten the nose at about 65 mph," Larry advises, "and just let her fly herself off."

We do as directed and this procedure requires twelve seconds from the time we began to roll. But we are light and, despite the heat, the V35A is indicating 1,000 fpm and 110 mph as we climb through 4,000 feet.

"Best angle of climb is at 80 mph," Larry says, "and best rate of climb at about 115 mph. Although control feel is very solid at 80, most people seem uncomfortable in such a steep attitude, and of course you give up much of the Bonanza's excellent over-the-nose visibility there. I prefer the cruise-climb which is 500 feet per minute and whatever air speed that produces—ordinarily, that'll build up to about 140 mph."

We continue upward, indicating 900 fpm as we pass through 5,000. Manifold pressure bottoms-out at 22 inches climbing through 6,500 feet. We go a few feet beyond and then nose down slightly to trim-out on the step at exactly 6,500. This gives us an indicated air speed of 175 mph at 2,500 rpm and 75% power. Outside air temp is 70 degrees F, and the fuel-flow meter shows 15.5 gallons per hour. We don't bother with our E-6B, but the old "add two percent per thousand feet" rule, figured in our head, tells us our true air speed is roughly 198 mph. A more precise calculation, feeding altitude and temp into the E-6B, would undoubtedly confirm the actual 203 mph TAS that Beech claims for these conditions.

"One thing I'd like to do now," Larry says, "is dispel some of that talk about the V-tail's allegedly poor spiral stability. We're in cruise configuration. Now let's give her a little up-trim and roll into a thirty-degree bank. Okay, now hands off the wheel, feet off the rudders, and let her ride around."

We watch apprehensively as the nose steepens into the spiral. There is some oscillation, and slowly the speed begins to build. However, the speed build-up is not at all rapid, nor does the nose continue to drop very much after a full minute and 360 degrees of turn hands off. Clearly, you would have to be sound asleep to allow the Bonanza V-tail to get away from you this way.

We level off and return to cruise and Larry has another goodie for us. "We're real proud of the Bonanza's speed versatility," he says. "It can fly with the Cubs or fly with the jets. We can fly the Bonanza at 175 mph in control zones and hold that speed right on final approach—you can actually do that right to the middle marker if you want to, because the Bonanza will then slow down to 100 mph in less than 20 seconds."

"Okay," we reply, "let's time it." We swing the wheel over to Larry and set the sweep hand on our stop watch at zero. "Ready? Go."

Larry cuts the throttle and flips down the landing gear knob (maximum gear-down speed is 175 mph in the V35A). A few seconds after that the air speed needle is unwinding through 150 mph as he gives it partial flaps (maximum flaps-down speed is 140 mph), and after a few more seconds he gives it full flaps as the needle backs through 140. At 100 mph, we push the button on our watch and take the reading. "Exactly 17 seconds," we announce.

Larry nods, satisfied, and demonstrates some stalls. He does the first one clean, power off and with feet on the floor. The stall-warning horn begins beeping at 70 and the break comes at 64 mph after the Bonanza's usual tail buffet. Wheel alone keeps the wings level and we recover straight ahead. "I didn't use half the aileron I had—there was plenty left," he said. "There's four degrees twist in the wings from the root to the tip of each, and that moves the stall out clear past the wing. That's also why you have the solid, big-airplane feel at 80 and 90 mph in this airplane; no mushy feeling even in 45 degree banks at 90."

Our next stall was done from slow flight with some power and gear and flaps down. It seemed to take forever, and the horn begins to irritate after 30 or 40 seconds of steady beeping. Meanwhile we play with the ailerons, enchanted at the degree of control we have at a little over 50 mph indicated. After a good deal of shaking, she at last quits flying at 50 mph.

We try the V35A's rapid descent ability, folding down the landing gear from cruise of 175 mph. We chop power and nose over and initial rate of descent leaps to 6,000 fpm. Then it unwinds to about 3,300 fpm with the air speed stabilized at 175. Descent attitude is very steep at this speed. There is of course some forward wheel left—probably enough for an outside loop—but in a sustained descent 3,300 fpm appears the maximum if you honor the 175 mph maximum gear-down speed. (The V35A owner's manual says you may lower the gear up to 200 mph in an emergency, although it may result in some damage to the gear doors.)

Larry then reminds us of the Bonanza's (all models) ability to safely bring a non-instrument pilot down through an undercast—with proper clearance from air traffic controllers, of course. "You know from previous experience with Bonanzas that all you have to do is put down the landing gear, establish a 500 fpm let-down, keep hands off the wheel and maintain heading with rudder alone," he reviews. "Now, suppose you've got turbulence; just how much control have you got in this configuration with rudder alone? Well, watch this."

Larry backs off some power and trims for a 500 fpm descent with the landing gear down and the air speed reading 100 mph. Then he reaches for the wheel and rolls us into a 30-degree left bank. He releases the wheel and rights the plane with rudder alone. There is some oscillation, but the control is positive and the wings return to level attitude. He repeats this demonstration to the right and again rudder alone picks up the wing. Then he does the same thing rolling from 45-degrees bank left to 45-degrees bank right and back to wings level—all with rudder-recovery alone. In the steeper banks some porpoising is noticeable in addition to the oscillation. Nevertheless, we always end up with wings level and the 500 fpm descent again stabilized. It's a pretty impressive demonstration.

We then experiment with glides, and although we don't carry one all the way to low altitude in order to check the V35A's advertised 12-to-1 glide ratio, we do note that at the Bonanza's best gliding speed of 90 mph rate-of-descent is 600 fpm at our loading.

Finally, we shoot some landings at Newton Municipal, but there's little to add in this department that hasn't already been said. She lands like a Bonanza—like all Bonanzas—and is easy to handle on the ground. The nose wheel deflects 17 degrees in either direction with rudder pressure alone.

Operating Costs. In the following estimated operating costs, gasoline is figured at 40¢ per gallon at a consumption rate of 13.4 gph (65% cruise power), engine exchange is assumed at 1,500 hours,

"Standard" V-tailed Bonanza is still queen of the single-engine Beechcrafts more than twenty years after the first one appeared.

hangar rental is based on a national average cost of $420 per year; operating cost per mile is based on a block speed of 190 mph, and seat-mile cost is based on an average utilization of four seats. Insurance includes hull and public liability (100,000/300,000), passenger liability (100,000/400,000) and property damage (100,-000). Premiums are based on rates obtainable under Beech finance plans and at an aircraft evaluation of $41,090 ($36,850 standard airplane plus $4,240 optional equipment).

Direct operating costs per hour

Gasoline	$ 5.36
Oil	.35
Inspection, maintenance & prop overhaul	3.80
Engine exchange allowance	2.92
Total Direct Operating Cost Per Hour	$12.43

Indirect operating costs

Hangar rent	$ 1.05
Insurance (based on 400 hrs. a year operation)	3.51
Total indirect operating cost per hour	$ 4.56
Total operating cost per hour	$16.99
Operating cost per mile	$ .089
Cost per seat mile	$ .022

Tax Savings. The tax savings you will earn with any corporate or company-owned airplane will help you cut cost in half. To illustrate how tax savings reduce cost of ownership, let's assume 1) that your company has an annual taxable income exceeding $25,000 subject to a tax rate of 53% (including basic tax rate and surcharge); and 2) that you are buying a Model V35A Bonanza new for $41,090 including $4,240 in optional equipment; and 3) that your company depreciates the airplane over a five-year period to a residual value of $8,218 (20% of purchase price):

Original purchase price	$41,090
Less tax savings over a 5-year period	17,422
Cost before investment tax credit	23,668
Less investment tax credit savings (2-1/3%)	959
Cost of airplane after 5 years	22,709
Less book value of plane (20% of purchase price)	8,218
Ultimate cost of airplane	$14,491

If your company has utilized the plane an average of 400 hours (76,000 miles) per year, then the cost for ownership is slightly over $7 per hour, or 3¢ per mile.

Just for kicks we figured the cost per mile for ownership of our Buick Sport Wagon and it came to 5¢ per mile (we paid $4,300 for it; will drive it about 50,000 miles in three years and then trade it, receiving, the dealer tells us, about $1,800 trade-in. Thus it costs about $2,500 to own for 50,000 miles). Operating cost per mile of the auto certainly won't beat the Bonanza's 9¢.

Of course, you can't take the Bonanza to the corner grocery for a quart of milk, and it's unrealistic to compare two different forms of transportation; the two machines are used for different tasks. We mention this only to point up the fact that a company-owned airplane in the Bonanza class can move key personnel at airline speeds (and on a schedule determined by the company) at an ultimate cost comparing favorably with that of a family car.

Leasing and Financing. A typical five-year leasing plan on a new Bonanza follows. You have the option of applying lease payments toward purchase at any time before the 48th payment is made:

Total cost of airplane including optional equipment $41,090
Security deposit required 6,163
Average monthly lease payment before tax saving (includes hull insurance reserve and $2 million single limit liability insurance reserve) 837
Average monthly lease payment after tax savings
(assume company is in the 53% tax bracket) .... $ 393

A typical 4-year financing plan, designed for use with the depreciation method most favorable to your company and based on a down payment of 25%, would look about like this:

Total cost of airplane including optional equipment $41,090
Down payment 10,272
Average monthly payment before tax savings, including hull insurance reserve 867
Average monthly payment after tax savings
(assumes company is in the 53% tax bracket) .... $ 460

v35a SPECIFICATIONS AND PERFORMANCE

Number of seats ....Four to six
Engine ....One Continental IO-520-B fuel injection, six-cylinder
Propeller ....Aluminum alloy blades, hydraulically controlled continuously variable pitch with spinner and hydraulic governor

Flight controls .... Single column, throw-over

Construction .... All metal

Landing gear .... Electrically retractable tricycle with swiveling nose wheel, shimmy dampener, oil-air struts

All-weather equipment .... Heated pitot tube

Cabin equipment .... Heater-defroster

Oxygen .... Optional

Application .... The Beechcraft Bonanza V35A is a four- to six-place, high performance, low-wing monoplane licensed in the utility category at full gross weight.

Engine .... Continental IO-520-B six-cylinder, fuel injection engine rated at 285 horsepower at 2,700 rpm for all operations.

Performance

High speed at sea level: (2,700 rpm, full throttle) .. 182 knots/210 mph

Cruising speeds:

· 75% power (2,500 rpm at 6,500 feet) .... 176 knots/203 mph

65% power (2,500 rpm at 10,000 feet) .... 172 knots/198 mph

45% power (2,300 rpm at 12,000 feet) .... 142 knots/164 mph

Rate of climb: (sea level)

285 rated horsepower .... 1,136 feet per minute

Service ceiling .... 17,500 feet

Absolute ceiling .... 19,200 feet

Stall speed (power off)

Gear down and flaps 30 degrees .... 55 knots/63 mph

Gear and flaps up .... 64 knots/74 mph

Take-off distance: (flaps 20 degrees)

Ground run .... 965 feet

Total over 50-foot-high obstacle .... 1,320 feet

Landing distance: (flaps 30 degrees)

Ground run .... 647 feet

Total over 50-foot-high obstacle .... 1,177 feet

Range: Includes warm-up, taxi, climb to altitude and 45-minutes reserve. Reserve computed at 45% power. Total optional tanks 80 gallons. Total standard tanks 50 gallons.

45% power at 12,000 feet .... standard tanks 599 miles

optional tanks 1,111 miles

65% power at 10,000 feet .... standard tanks 539 miles

optional tanks 989 miles

75% power at 6,500 feet .... standard tanks 495 miles

optional tanks 896 miles

Weights

Gross weight .... 3,400 pounds

Empty weight (includes 21 pounds avionics) .... 1,958 pounds

Useful load (standard tank full) .... 1,442 pounds

Baggage .... 270 pounds

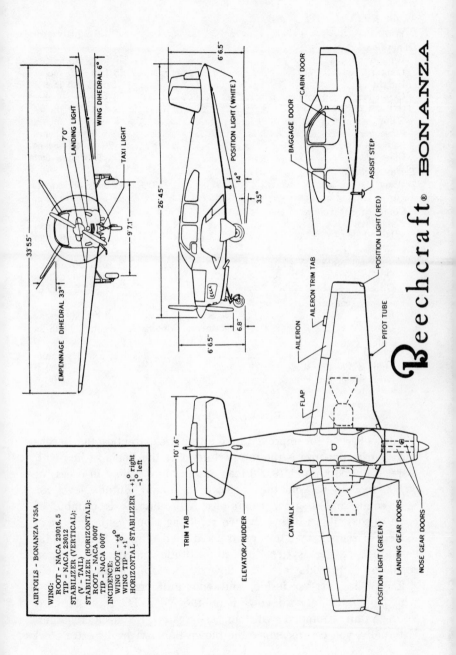

AIRFOILS - BONANZA V35A

WING:
ROOT - NACA 23016.5
TIP - NACA 23012
STABILIZER (VERTICAL):
(V - TAIL)
STABILIZER (HORIZONTAL):
ROOT - NACA 0007
TIP - NACA 0007
INCIDENCE:
WING ROOT - +4°
WING TIP - +1°
HORIZONTAL STABILIZER - +1° right
-1° left

EMPENNAGE DIHEDRAL 33°

WING DIHEDRAL 6°

33'5.5"

7'0"

LANDING LIGHT

TAXI LIGHT

9'7.1"

26'4.5"

6'6.5"

POSITION LIGHT (WHITE)

14°

3.5°

6'6.5"

6.8"

CABIN DOOR

BAGGAGE DOOR

ASSIST STEP

POSITION LIGHT (RED)

PITOT TUBE

AILERON TRIM TAB

AILERON

FLAP

10'1.6"

TRIM TAB

ELEVATOR/RUDDER

CATWALK

POSITION LIGHT (GREEN)

LANDING GEAR DOORS

NOSE GEAR DOORS

D

Beechcraft® BONANZA

Areas

Wing .... 181.0 square feet

Dimensions

Wing span .... 33 feet, 5.5 inches
Length .... 26 feet, 4.5 inches
Height .... 6 feet, 6.5 inches
Cabin length (instrument panel aft) .... 8 feet, 6 inches
Cabin width .... 3 feet, 6 inches
Cabin height .... 4 feet, 2 inches
Passenger door size .... 36 by 37 inches
Baggage door size .... 20 by 24 inches
Glass area .... 27 square feet

Technical data

Wing loading at gross weight .... 18.78 pounds per sq. ft.
Power loading at gross weight .... 11.93 pounds per hp.

Compartment volume
Baggage .... 35.0 cubic feet
Hat shelf .... 1.7 cubic feet

Fuel capacity
Standard tanks .... Total 50 gallons
Optional tanks .... Total 80 gallons
Oil .... 3 gallons

Fuel specifications
Fuel .... 100/130 octane
Oil .... Continental Motors Specification MHS-24

Landing gear
Brakes .... Hydraulic
Main wheel tire size 7.00–6
Nose wheel tire size 5.00–5

BONANZA V35A-TC

Turbocharged for improved high altitude capabilities, the Beech-craft Turbo Bonanza is the top performer of the Bonanza line with a speed of 250 mph at 19,000 feet. An absolute ceiling in excess of 30,000 feet allows you the choice of optimum altitude level for best winds and weather conditions. This aircraft is capable of coast-to-coast flight with only two refueling stops (although we're moved to remark that few pilots have such range). Standard 49-cubic-foot oxygen system has an altitude-compensated oxygen regulator to provide increased flow at increased altitude.

Except for oxygen inside, and one additional control knob—which operates forward cowl flaps—the V35A-TC is a standard V35A V-tail equipped with an AiResearch turbo-supercharger. Externally, you can recognize the blown-Bonanza by its extra cowl

Bonanza V35A-TC is turbocharged for speeds to 250 mph at 19,000 feet. Most noticeable external difference is its single exhaust.

flap on each side of the nose, its single exhaust, and of course the legend, "Turbocharged 285" lettered on the cowling.

Our colleague, aviation writer and long-time Bonanza owner Page Shamburger, had recently flown a turbocharged V-tail, so we asked Page to give us her impressions of it. Page has been flying for 25 years and has 5,000 hours logged, a significant proportion of that time in earlier Bonanzas.

"First of all," Page said, "normally aspirated Bonanzas perform best at 6,500 feet, at which altitude you've already given up 25% of your power. The TC Bonanza, however, furnishes full sea level-type power right up to 16,000. I held 1,000 fpm climb through 12,000; indicated 700 fpm going through 18,000, and reached 25,000 feet in less than 22 minutes from take-off. Up there, the winds are big, the weather little, and the boosted-Bonanza goes like suddenly. You can true-out at 220 mph using only 65% power at 2,500 rpm. Or, you can spend 75% power at that altitude and get 230 mph; and up there, where you can see all the way to tomorrow, turbulence bounces you only seldomly. Add to all that your very excellent chance of finding a friendly 60 mph tailwind, especially on an easterly heading, and you are right at home with the big guys.

"You can make this fast climb to altitude in the TC Bonanza because its dash-D engine has no manifold-pressure restrictions. The Continental IO-520-D in the TC has a compression ratio of

7.5 : 1 (while the IO-520-B used in the V35A has 8.5 : 1), and this eliminates the possibility of detonation at the high induction air temperatures of the turbo installation. This allows high manifold pressures. For example, with the normally aspirated engine at sea level, manifold pressure is 29.6 inches at 2,700 rpm (full power), while you pull 32.5 inches at 2,700 rpm with the blower. And you can hold this 32.5 inches just as high as it'll go.

"I climbed the TC Bonanza at 28 inches and 2,500 rpm, which is about 85% power. I put on the oxygen mask at 10,000, and was reminded that there'd be no smoking from that point. Above 18,000, altimeter settings go to 29.92 (standard atmosphere) and you must be transponder-equipped and file a flight plan.

"In sum, I'd say the difference comes on hot days at all altitudes; and it comes any day up high where the TC Bonanza likes to go far and fast. As for handling, well, that's standard Bonanza."

Operating Costs. In the following estimated operating costs, gasoline consumption is based upon an average flight of two hours, with climb-fuel calculated at 85% power, 20.3 gph, and cruise fuel at 65% power, 13.7 gph. Average consumption 15 gph at 40¢ per gallon. Engine exchange allowance and turbocharger overhaul provides a reserve for 1,400-hour engine exchange. Insurance includes hull and public liability (100,000/300,000), passenger liability (100,000/400,000), and property damage (100,000). Operating cost per mile is based on a block speed of 205 mph, and cost per seat mile assumes average utilization of four seats:

Direct operating cost per hour
Gasoline	$ 6.00
Oil	.35
Inspection, maintenance & prop overhaul	3.97
Engine exchange & turbocharger overhaul	4.90
Total direct operating cost per hour	$15.22

Indirect operating costs
Hangar rental	$ 1.05
Insurance	3.98
Total indirect operating cost per hour (based on 400 hours per year operation)	$ 5.03
Total operating cost per hour	$20.25
Operating cost per mile	$ .099
Cost per seat mile	$ .025

Tax Savings. If your company has an annual taxable income exceeding $25,000 subject to a tax rate of 53% (including basic tax rate and surcharge), actual cost of a typical V35A-TC might be computed as follows, assuming your company depreciates the airplane over a five-year period to a residual value of 20% of purchase price:

Original price including $4,600 opt. equipment	$47,350
Less tax savings over a five-year period	20,076
Cost before investment tax credit	27,274
Less investment tax credit saving (2–1/3%)	1,105
Cost after five years	26,169
Less book value of plane (20% of purchase price)	9,470
Ultimate cost of airplane	$16,699

Leasing and financing plans for V35A-TC Bonanza acquisition are similar to those explained for the V35A.

v35a-tc BONANZA PERFORMANCE & SPECIFICATIONS

Engine: Continental TSIO-520-D turbo-charged, six-cylinder, fuel injection engine rated at 285 horsepower at 2,700 rpm for all operations.

Performance

High speed at 19,000 feet	217 knots/250 mph
Cruising speeds:	
75% power (2,500 rpm @ 24,000 feet)	200 knots/230 mph
(2,500 rpm @ 6,500 feet)	176 knots/203 mph
65% power (2,500 rpm @ 27,000 feet)	192 knots/221 mph
(2,300 rpm @ 10,000 feet)	171 knots/197 mph
45% power (2,200 rpm @ 16,000 feet)	144 knots/166 mph
Rate of climb: (sea level)	
285 rated horsepower	1,225 feet per minute
Service ceiling	29,500 feet
Absolute ceiling	30,700 feet
Stall speed (power off)	
Gear down, flaps 30 degrees	55 knots/63 mph
Gear and flaps up	64 knots/74 mph
Take-off distance (flaps 20 degrees)	
Ground run	950 feet
Total over 50-foot-high obstacle	1,320 feet
Landing distance (flaps 30 degrees)	
Ground run	647 feet
Total over 50-foot-high obstacle	1,177 feet

Range: Include warm-up, taxi, climb to altitude with 45-minute reserve. Reserve computed at 45% power. Total 80 gallons optional tanks. 50 gallons standard tanks.

45% power at 16,000 feet		standard tanks	574	miles
		optional tanks	1,082	miles
65% power at 10,000 feet		standard tanks	512	miles
		optional tanks	944	miles
	27,000 feet	standard tanks	519	miles
		optional tanks	1,020	miles
75% power at 6,500 feet		standard tanks	473	miles
		optional tanks	860	miles
	24,000 feet	standard tanks	494	miles
		optional tanks	950	miles

Weights

Gross weight .... 3,400 pounds
Empty weight (includes 21 pounds avionics) .... 2,021 pounds
Useful load with standard tanks full .... 1,379 pounds
Baggage .... 270 pounds

Areas:

Wing .... 181.0 square feet

Dimensions:

Wing span .... 33 feet, 5.5 inches
Length .... 26 feet, 4.5 inches
Height .... 6 feet, 6.5 inches
Cabin length (instrument panel aft) .... 8 feet, 6 inches
Cabin width .... 3 feet, 6 inches
Cabin height .... 4 feet, 2 inches
Passenger door size .... 36 by 37 inches
Baggage door size .... 20 by 24 inches
Glass area .... 27 square feet

Technical Data:

Wing loading at gross weight .... 18.78 pounds per square foot
Power loading at gross weight .... 11.93 pounds per horsepower
Compartment volume
  Baggage .... 35.0 cubic feet
  Hat shelf .... 1.7 cubic feet
Fuel capacity
  Standard tanks .... Total 50 gallons
  Optional tanks .... Total 80 gallons
  Oil .... 3 gallons
Fuel specifications
  Fuel .... 100/130 octane
  Oil .... Continental Motors Specifications MHS-24
Landing gear
  Brakes .... Hydraulic
  Main wheel tire size 7.00–6
  Nose wheel tire size 5.00–5
Oxygen .... 49-cubic-feet standard

BONANZA MODEL 36

Aimed at the utility aircraft market, the Bonanza 36, with a top speed of 204 mph and a range of nearly 1,000 miles (including reserves), will accommodate six passengers or a useful load of 1,620 lbs. Introduced in 1968, the Bonanza 36 is licensed in the utility category at full gross weight of 3,600 lbs. It is ten inches longer than other Bonanzas, and double doors on the starboard side just aft of the wing provide a twelve square-foot opening (regular cabin door forward is of course retained) to make easy the handling of bulky cargo and stretcher patients. The Model 36 is, simply, an aerial station wagon. And the addition of six cubic feet in the cabin has added but 31 pounds to the Bonanza's empty weight.

The "big" Bonanza Model 36 with lengthened fuselage and large double doors aft of wing was introduced in 1968.

This craft has the Model 33's conventional tail and, except for the cabin modification, is otherwise standard Bonanza. Those big doors aft employ bonded honeycomb construction to insure strength and fit and are designed so they cannot be latched unless fully closed. A warning indicator on the instrument panel signals the pilot when these doors are not securely closed and locked.

A typical air-taxi mission for the 36 could include pilot, five passengers, 140 pounds of baggage, and full (optional) fuel tanks of 80 gallons in all-weather operation. Interior conversion from passenger to cargo configuration is fast and easy.

Three interior option packages include a choice of four fabrics, two vinyls, two headliner, and five carpet, seatbelt, and scuff-panel colors. Deluxe interiors offer a choice of seven leathers and five

Krollpoint fabrics. Heavy duty utility interiors are available in breathable vinyls.

A standard avionics package includes 360-channel transceiver, 100-channel nav receiver, navigation converter-indicator (Omni), and accessories.

Individual windows, fresh air inlets, and reading lights are available at each passenger position. Seats are fully adjustable with reclining backs; and fifth and sixth cabin seats fold rearward while third and fourth seats have quick-release pins for removal when converting the Model 36 to utility configuration.

Suggested selling price is $40,650.

The Model 36 gives up six mph top speed and five to eight mph at cruise in exchange for its extra cabin capacity and conventional tail when compared with the V-tailed standard Bonanza; but this seems a pretty good trade if your requirements dictate an airplane with more utility potential than possessed by the "standard" Bonanza.

Speaking of "standard" Bonanzas, that really isn't a very good term for them. All Bonanzas are custom built to a significant degree. In addition to interior leathers and fabrics (or vinyls), each Bonanza buyer chooses his own paint job (that is, choice of colors), and his own instrument and avionics packages as well as other options including tip tanks, automatic wing leveller, etc. It is therefore highly improbable that two Bonanzas exactly alike will leave the production line during the production-life of any model.

Except for the slight speed penalty, the Bonanza 36 performs like any other conventional-tailed Bonanza—which is to say, like all Bonanzas generally (in its horsepower class). With 600 pounds of people and full optional tanks (80 gal) we indicated a 1,450 fpm rate of climb just after take-off on a 94 degree F day. Indicated air speed was 120 mph and we were showing 25 inches of mercury, 2,500 rpms and a fuel consumption rate of 21 gph. A 500 fpm climb resulted in an indicated air speed of 155 mph.

Trimming-out at 6,500 feet, we check outside air temp at 75 degrees F. With 2,500 rpm and slightly over 23 inches of manifold pressure, we indicate 176 mph with the fuel flow meter down to 15 gallons per hour. Again, we don't bother with our pocket computer, but adding 2% per thousand feet a la Travel Air days, arrive at a true air speed of 199 mph. If you want to check our helmet-and-goggle type figure on your own computer, the figures are there: 75 degrees, 6,500 pressure altitude and 176 IAS. Beech claims 195 mph (170 knots) for 2,500 rpm and 6,500 feet.

Stall speed, power off and clean, is 72 mph. With gear and flaps down and some power, you can fly her down to slightly under 50. Power off, gear and flaps down, the stall comes at 63 to 64 mph. In slow flight at 60–65 mph, the 36 retains a solid feel, and 30-degree banked turns produce no mushiness. Larry Long told us he had flown a photographic mission with a J-3 Cub a few days before, and said he had spent an hour and a half in the 36 holding 60 mph while two photographers shot pictures from the big opening aft with the double doors removed.

Bonanza 36 was designed for the utility market, primarily as an air taxi/cargo craft. Engine is 285 hp Continental; top speed, 204 mph. Range, with reserves, 980 miles.

Landing the 36 is normal. Lower the landing gear on downwind leg roughly opposite your touch-down point, then ease back power and trim for 500 fpm rate of descent at 100 mph. Lower flaps—if you want them—in base leg, then you may fly final somewhere between 80 and 90 as it suits you. Final power reduction comes with the flare-out.

Operating Costs. In the following estimated operating costs, gasoline is figured at 40¢ per gallon at a consumption rate of 13.4 gph (65% cruise power), engine exchange is assumed at 1,500 hours, hangar rental is based on the national average cost of $420 per year; operating cost per mile is based on a block speed of 182 mph, and seat-mile cost is based on an average utilization of six seats. Insurance includes hull and public liability (100,000/300,000), passenger liability (100,000/300,000), and property damage (100,-000). Premiums are based on rates obtainable under Beech finance plans and at an aircraft evaluation of $45,515 ($40,650 standard airplane plus $4,865 optional equipment).

Direct operating costs per hour

Gasoline	$5.36
Oil	.35
Inspection, maintenance & prop overhaul	$3.80
Engine exchange allowance	2.92
Total direct operating cost per hour	$12.43

Indirect operating costs

Hangar rent	$ 1.05
Insurance	3.98
(Based on 400 hours per year operation)	
Total indirect operating cost per hour	$ 5.03
Total operating cost per hour	$17.46
Operating cost per mile	$ .096
Cost per seat mile	$ .016

Tax Savings. The tax savings you will earn with 36 Bonanza ownership will help you cut all your costs in half. To illustrate how this works let's assume 1) that your company has an annual taxable income exceeding $25,000 subject to a tax rate of 53% (including basic tax rate and surcharge); 2) that you are buying a Model 35 Bonanza for $45,515 including $4,865 optional equipment; and 3) that your company depreciates the airplane over a five-year period to a residual value of $9,103 (20% of purchase price):

Original purchase price	$45,515
Less tax saving over a 5-year period	19,298
Cost before investment tax credit	26,217
Less investment tax credit savings (2⅓%)	1,062
Cost of airplane after five years	$25,155
Less book value of plane (20% of purchase price)	9,013
Ultimate cost of airplane	$16,052

If your company has utilized this craft an average of 400 hours per year during this five-year period, the cost of ownership is $8.02 per hour. Therefore, total cost of ownership and operation (assuming operating costs are totally tax deductible as a business expense) is roughly $16.50 per hour.

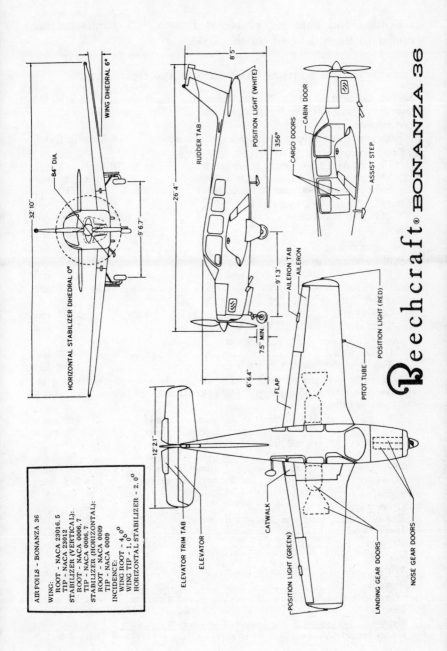

AIR FOILS - BONANZA 36

WING:
  ROOT - NACA 23016.5
  TIP - NACA 23012
STABILIZER (VERTICAL):
  ROOT - NACA 0006.7
  TIP - NACA 0006.7
STABILIZER (HORIZONTAL):
  ROOT - NACA 0009
  TIP - NACA 0009
INCIDENCE:
  WING ROOT - 4.0°
  WING TIP - 1.0°
  HORIZONTAL STABILIZER - 2.0°

WING DIHEDRAL 6°

HORIZONTAL STABILIZER DIHEDRAL 0°

84" DIA.

32' 10"

9' 6.7"

26' 4"

9' 1.3"

7.5" MIN

6' 4"

8' 5"

356°

RUDDER TAB

POSITION LIGHT (WHITE)

CARGO DOORS

CABIN DOOR

ASSIST STEP

AILERON TAB

AILERON

POSITION LIGHT (RED)

FLAP

PITOT TUBE

12' 2.1"

ELEVATOR TRIM TAB

ELEVATOR

CATWALK

POSITION LIGHT (GREEN)

LANDING GEAR DOORS

NOSE GEAR DOORS

Beechcraft® BONANZA 36

101

Leasing and financing plans for Bonanza 36 acquisition are similar to those detailed for the V35A.

MODEL 36 BONANZA PERFORMANCE AND SPECIFICATIONS

Engine: Continental IO-520-B six-cylinder, fuel injection engine rated at 285 horsepower at 2,700 rpm for all operations.

Performance

    High speed at sea level (2,700 rpm, full throttle) .. 178 knots/204 mph

    Cruising speeds
        75% power (2,500 rpm at 6,500 feet) .... 170 knots/195 mph
        65% power (2,500 rpm at 10,000 feet) .... 162 knots/187 mph
        55% power (2,300 rpm at 10,000 feet) .... 145 knots/167 mph

    Rate of climb: (sea level)
        285 rated horsepower .... 1,015 feet per minute

    Service ceiling .... 16,000 feet

    Absolute ceiling .... 17,800 feet

    Stall speed (power off)
        Gear down and flaps 30 degrees .... 56 knots/64 mph
        Gear and flaps up .... 65 knots/75 mph

    Take-off distance (flaps 20 degrees)
        Ground run .... 1,112 feet
        Total over 50-foot-high obstacle .... 1,525 feet

    Landing distance (flaps 30 degrees)
        Ground run .... 683 feet
        Total over 50-foot-high obstacle .... 1,240 feet

Range: Includes warm-up, taxi, climb to altitude and 45-minutes reserve. Reserve computed at 45% power. Total optional tanks 80 gallons. Total standard tanks 50 gallons.

55% power at 10,000 feet	standard tanks	530 miles
	optional tanks	980 miles
65% power at 10,000 feet	standard tanks	515 miles
	optional tanks	945 miles
75% power at 6,500 feet	standard tanks	485 miles
	optional tanks	875 miles

Weights

    Gross weight .... 3,600 pounds
    Empty weight (includes 25 pounds avionics) .... 1,980 pounds
    Useful load .... 1,620 pounds
    Baggage .... 400 pounds

Areas

    Wing .... 177.6 square feet

Dimensions

    Wing span .... 32 feet, 10 inches
    Length .... 26 feet, 4 inches
    Height .... 8 feet, 5 inches
    Cabin length .... 9 feet, 4 inches

Cabin width .... 3 feet, 6 inches
Cabin height .... 4 feet, 2 inches
Forward passenger door size .... 36 by 27 inches
Rear passenger door size .... 40 by 45 inches
Glass area .... 28 square feet

Technical data
Wing loading at gross weight .... 20.2 pounds per square foot
Power loading at gross weight .... 12.6 pounds per horsepower
Compartment volume
    Baggage (aft of third and fourth seats) .... 40.0 cubic feet

Fuel capacity
    Standard tanks .... Total 50 gallons
    Optional tanks .... Total 80 gallons
    Oil .... 3 gallons

Fuel specifications
    Fuel .... 100/130 octane
    Oil .... Continental Motors Specification MHS-24

Landing gear
    Brakes .... Hydraulic
    Main wheel tire size 7.00–6
    Nose wheel tire size 5.00–5

E33A, E33, E33B, E33C BONANZA SERIES

The Bonanza Model 33 (née Debonair) is, as previously noted, essentially the same airplane as the Model 35 Series except for its conventional tail. A swept rudder was the only thing Beech engineers had to design for addition to a standard V-tail airframe. The Model 33 Series' horizontal tail surfaces—stronger than needed and well tested—were simply borrowed from the T-34 Beechcraft Mentor.

The four airplanes offered in the Model 33 Series are the 225 hp E33, the 285 hp E33A, and aerobatic versions of each which are called the E33B (225 hp) and the E33C (285 hp).

The Akro versions were introduced late in 1968, and are licensed for such maneuvers as rolls, inside loops, Immelmann turns, Cuban-eights, split-S, snap rolls, spins, and limited inverted flight. Beech says development of aerobatic versions of the Bonanza was called for because of increasing international emphasis on unusual-attitude recovery in civilian, military, and airline flight training programs, plus the growing number of pilots who find recreation in akro-flying. And the Beechcraft E33B and E33C are the first business aircraft to offer true sport flying with no sacrifice in

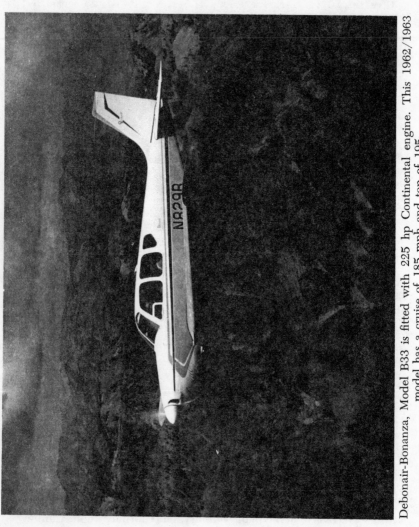

Debonair-Bonanza, Model B33 is fitted with 225 hp Continental engine. This 1962/1963 model has a cruise of 185 mph and top of 195.

utility. Both retain the standard four to five place interior with a useful load in the utility category of about 1,196 pounds for the 225 hp E33B, and 1,400 pounds for the 285 hp E33C.

Operation in aerobatic category is limited to pilot and one passenger.

Structural changes made to obtain aerobatic licensing under FAR Part 3 included the addition of aft fuselage structural members and some beefing-up of ailerons, all tail surfaces, and installation of larger rudder cables.

Standard equipment on the aerobatic models includes shoulder harness for two front seats, quick-release cabin door, and a G-meter on the instrument panel. Checkerboard wing-tips and rudder stripe identify the akro-Bonanzas.

Suggested selling price, including standard instruments and avionics, for the aerobatic Bonanzas, was, in 1969, $34,250 for the E33B, and $38,250 for the E33C.

Suggested selling price in 1969 of the E33 (with standard instruments and avionics), was $31,750; and 1969 price of the similarly equipped E33A was $35,750.

Specifications and performance figures are, of course, almost identical for the 225 hp Bonanza, whether aerobatic or not, and regardless of year model. The 225 hp aerobatic Bonanza has an empty weight 23 pounds greater than the E33 (and matching loss in useful load); otherwise the specs are the same. Also, comparing

Bonanza E33, 1968/1969 model, has large rear window, ventral fin, one-piece windshield and other goodies, but performance, with 225 hp Continental engine, is comparable to earlier Debonair of same horsepower.

specs of the 1969 Model E33 with those of the 1962 B33, you'll find no significant differences—except that the airplane has grown slightly heavier and given up some of its useful load as a result.

The same thing applies to other Bonanzas including the 285 hp models in the 33 Series. Clearly, when you start out with a good design, well thought out and exhaustively tested, there isn't much you can do to it except posh it up a little, change the paint job, and adjust the price upwards to keep up with an inflating economy.

There's nothing wrong with such a policy. Rolls-Royce has practiced it for years in the automobile market. American car makers

Bonanza E33A is fitted with 285 hp Continental which gives it a top speed of 208 mph. Range, with reserves, is 1,080 miles.

render our automobiles obsolete by popularizing new external shapes year by year while mechanically there has been small improvement in a decade. (Our 1941 Buick would do 100 mph. We had power brakes on a 1932 Nash; hydraulic brakes on a 1925 Dodge.) But you can't arbitrarily change the external shape of an airplane without changing its flight characteristics; therefore, style and year-model cannot be considered a function of aircraft shape. Since the laws of aerodynamics do not change from year to year, neither can the shapes which must obey those laws. By, say, 1960, the single-engined four-to-five-place retractable had been developed to its practical limit. Somewhere in the future we may build these aircraft of different materials and give them a different propulsion system. Meanwhile, at least for another decade or so, planes of this class will change little, except for paint, price and poshness.

Since there is almost no difference in the performance of a B33 (evaluated earlier in this book) and the E33, we won't give space to a demonstration flight here.

BONANZA E33 AND E33B (AEROBATIC) OPERATING COSTS

Direct operating cost per hour

Gasoline	$ 4.37
Oil	.42
Inspection, maintenance and prop overhaul	2.56
Engine exchange allowance	2.57
Total direct operating cost per hour	$ 9.92

Indirect Operating Costs

Hangar rent	$ 1.05
Insurance	3.14
Total indirect operating cost per hour	$ 4.19
Total operating cost per hour	$14.11
Operating cost per plane mile	.083
Cost per seat mile	.021

Above figures are based upon an average of 400 hours per year operation. Gasoline (80/87) was figured at a consumption rate of 11.5 gph and 38¢ per gallon, assuming aircraft operation at 65% cruise power and a block speed of 170 mph, with allowance for normal warm-up and climb to altitude. Engine exchange is computed at 1,500 hours. Insurance includes hull and public liability (100,000/300,000), passenger liability (100,000/300,000), and property damage (100,000). Premiums are based on rates obtainable under Beech finance plans and at an aircraft evaluation of $35,995 ($31,750 standard airplane, plus $4,245 optional equipment).

Tax Savings. Tax savings on an E33 will help cut costs in half if your company has an annual taxable income exceeding $25,000 subject to a tax rate of 53% (basic tax and surcharge). This assumes that your company-owned E33 Bonanza is purchased for $35,995 including $4,245 optional equipment, and that you depreciate the airplane over a five-year period to a residual value of $7,199 or 20% of the purchase price.

Bonanza E33 instrument panel with typical avionics installation.

Original price	$35,995
Less tax savings over a 5-year period	15,262
Cost before Investment Tax credit	20,733
Less Investment Tax credit	840
Cost after 5 years	19,893
Less book value of plane (20% of purchase price)	7,199
Ultimate cost of the airplane	$12,694

Leasing and Financing. Beech Acceptance Corporation, a subsidiary of Beech Aircraft, has a number of leasing and financing plans which include low group insurance rates. A five-year lease plan might look like this:

Original price including optional equipment	$35,995
Security deposit	5,399
Average monthly lease payment before taxes	735
Average payment after tax savings	345

These plans assume company ownership by a company in the 53% tax bracket.

And a typical four-year finance plan might look like this:

Original price including optional equipment	$35,995

Down payment (25%) 8,998
Average monthly payment before taxes 760
Average monthly payment after taxes 357
Insurance included in both of the above plans.

E33 AND E33B PERFORMANCE AND SPECIFICATIONS

Engine: Continental IO-470-K six-cylinder, fuel injection engine rated at 225 horsepower at 2,600 rpm for all operations.

Performance

High speed at sea level (2,600 rpm, full throttle) .. 170 knots/195 mph

Cruising speeds
  75% power (2,450 rmp at 7,000 feet) .... 161 knots/185 mph
  65% power (2,450 rpm at 11,000 feet) .... 156 knots/180 mph
  50% power (2,100 rpm at 11,000 feet) .... 134 knots/154 mph

Rate of climb (sea level)
  225 rated horsepower .... 930 feet per minute

Service ceiling .... 17,800 feet

Absolute ceiling .... 20,000 feet

Stall speed (power off)
  Gear down and flaps 30 degrees .... 52 knots/60 mph
  Gear and flaps up .... 61 knots/71 mph

Take-off distance (flaps 20 degrees)
  Ground run .... 982 feet
  Total over 50-foot-high obstacle .... 1,288 feet

Landing distance (flaps 30 degrees)
  Ground run .... 643 feet
  Total over 50-foot-high obstacle .... 1,298 feet

Range: Includes warm-up, taxi, climb to altitude and 45-minute reserve. Reserve computed at 45% power. Total optional tanks 80 gallons. Total standard tanks 50 gallons.

50% power at 7,000 feet	standard tanks	650 miles
	optional tanks	1,170 miles
65% power at 11,000 feet	standard tanks	595 miles
	optional tanks	1,075 miles
75% power at 7,000 feet	standard tanks	540 miles
	optional tanks	965 miles

Weights
  Gross weight .... 3,050 pounds
  Empty weight (includes 21 pounds avionics) .... 1,862 pounds
  Useful load .... 1,188 pounds
  Baggage .... 270 pounds

Areas
  Wing .... 177.6 square feet

Dimensions
  Wing span .... 32 feet, 10 inches
  Length .... 25 feet, 6 inches

```
Height ............................................  8 feet,  3 inches
Cabin length (instrument panel aft) ................  6 feet, 11 inches
Cabin width ......................................  3 feet,  6 inches
Cabin height .....................................  4 feet,  2 inches
Passenger door size ............................... 36 by 37 inches
Baggage door size ................................ 20 by 24 inches
```

Technical data

```
Wing loading at gross weight .............. 17.2 pounds per square foot
Power loading at gross weight ............. 13.5 pounds per horsepower
```

Compartment volume

```
Baggage ........................................ 20.0 cubic feet
Baggage with utility shelf ........................ 25.4 cubic feet
```

Fuel capacity

```
Standard tanks ................................. Total 50 gallons
Optional tanks ................................. Total 80 gallons
Oil ................................................ 2.5 gallons
```

Fuel specifications

```
Fuel .................................................. 80/87 octane
Oil ..................... Continental Motors Specification MHS-24
```

BONANZA E33A AND E33C PERFORMANCE AND SPECIFICATIONS

The 285 hp conventional-tailed Bonanzas have the same operating costs as the 285 hp V-tailed V35A listed previously, except for

Bonanza E33C is 285 hp aerobatic version of the E33A. It is licensed in Utility Category as a four or five-placer; is limited to two-place for akro-flight. The 225 hp E33 Bonanza becomes the E33B fitted for aerobatics.

a 9¢ per hour saving in insurance due to a $1,100 lower list price than the V-tail (the aerobatic E33C, however, lists for $1,400 more than the V35A). Difference in cost of ownership is negligible.

Performancewise, there are some differences, and a comparison of the following figures with those given for the V35A will reveal these subtle variations.

Engine: Continental IO-520-B six-cylinder, fuel injection engine rated at 285 horsepower at 2,700 rpm for all operations.

Performance

High speed at sea level (2,700 rpm, full throttle) .... 180 knots/208 mph

Cruising speeds
75% power (2,500 rpm at 6,500 feet) ....174 knots/200 mph
65% power (2,500 rpm at 10,000 feet) .... 169 knots/195 mph
45% power (2,300 rpm at 12,000 feet) .... 135 knots/156 mph

Rate of climb (sea level)
285 rated horsepower .... 1,200 feet per minute

Service ceiling .... 18,300 feet

Absolute ceiling .... 20,000 feet

Stall speed (power off)
Gear down and flaps 30 degrees .... 53 knots/61 mph
Gear and flaps up .... 63 knots/72 mph

Take-off Distance (flaps 20 degrees)
Ground run .... 880 feet
Total over 50-foot-high obstacle .... 1,225 feet

Landing distance (flap 30 degrees)
Ground run .... 625 feet
Total over 50-foot-high obstacle .... 1,150 feet

Range: Includes warm-up, taxi, climb to altitude and 45-minute reserve. Reserve computed at 45% power. Total optional tanks 80 gallons. Total standard tanks 50 gallons.

45% power at 10,000 feet	standard tanks		595 miles
	optional tanks		1,080 miles
65% power at 10,000 feet	standard tanks		535 miles
	optional tanks		981 miles
75% power at 6,500 feet	standard tanks		495 miles
	optional tanks		896 miles

Weights
Gross weight .... 3,300 pounds
Empty weight (includes 21 pounds avionics) .... 1,915 pounds
Useful load .... 1,385 pounds
Baggage .... 270 pounds

Areas
Wing .... 177.6 square feet

Dimensions
Wing span .... 32 feet, 10 inches
Length .... 25 feet, 6 inches

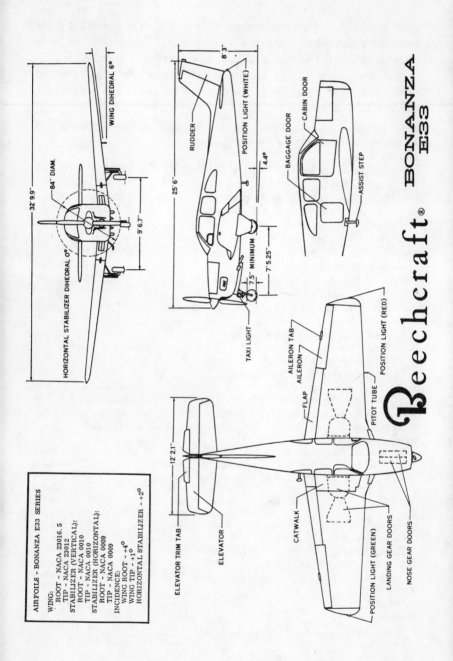

AIRFOILS - BONANZA E33 SERIES

WING:
ROOT - NACA 23016.5
TIP - NACA 23012
STABILIZER (VERTICAL):
ROOT - NACA 0010
TIP - NACA 0010
STABILIZER (HORIZONTAL):
ROOT - NACA 0009
TIP - NACA 0009
INCIDENCE:
WING ROOT - +4°
WING TIP - +1°
HORIZONTAL STABILIZER - +2°

WING DIHEDRAL 6°

HORIZONTAL STABILIZER DIHEDRAL 0°

32' 9.9"

84" DIAM.

9' 6.7"

8' 3"

RUDDER

POSITION LIGHT (WHITE)

25' 6"

1.4°

7.5" MINIMUM

7' 5.25"

TAXI LIGHT

BAGGAGE DOOR

CABIN DOOR

ASSIST STEP

ELEVATOR TRIM TAB

12' 2.1"

ELEVATOR

CATWALK

FLAP

AILERON TAB

AILERON

PITOT TUBE

POSITION LIGHT (RED)

POSITION LIGHT (GREEN)

LANDING GEAR DOORS

NOSE GEAR DOORS

Beechcraft® BONANZA E33

112

Height .... 8 feet, 3 inches
Cabin length (instrument panel aft) .... 6 feet, 11 inches
Cabin width .... 3 feet, 6 inches
Cabin height .... 4 feet, 2 inches
Passenger door size .... 36 by 37 inches
Baggage door size .... 20 by 24 inches
Glass area .... 27 square feet

Technical Data

Wing loading at gross weight .... 18.6 pounds per square foot
Power loading at gross weight .... 11.6 pounds per horsepower

Compartment volume
Baggage .... 20.0 cubic feet
Baggage with utility shelf .... 25.4 cubic feet

Fuel capacity
Standard tanks .... Total 50 gallons
Optional tanks .... Total 80 gallons
Oil .... 3 galllons

Fuel specifications
Fuel .... 100/130 octane
Oil .... Continental Motors
Specification MHS-24

Landing gear
Brakes .... Hydraulic
Main wheel tire size 6.00–9
Nose wheel tire size 5.00–5

7. Beechcraft Skipper

After a four-year gestation period, Beech finally put its little two-place, T-tailed trainer in production late in 1978 with first deliveries beginning early in 1979. The first ones, therefore, are 1979 models. Called the PD-285 during development, the new Model 77 is going to have to face the world as the "Skipper." Good grief. That must have come from the same character who thought up "Musketeer."

The Skipper is built at the Beech facility in Liberal, KS where the Sundowner and Sierra are produced (and the twin-engined Duchess). It is an all-new design intended as a functional, comfortable, private pilot trainer. A substantial part of the Skipper's construction is bonded metal, including the lower cabin section of the fuselage, the entire wing, the leading edge of the vertical stabilizer, a large portion of the horizontal stabilizer, the elevator trim tabs, and the rudder.

Employment of the T-tail and the NASA-developed GAW-1 wing combine for a smoother ride and more positive control when landing with the horizontal tail above the slipstream, and the airfoil shape used in the wing, an outgrowth of NASA's high-speed super-critical airfoil research, provides lower drag and higher lift than other airfoils suitable for small aircraft. Spin characteristics of this combination are excellent. The wing, by the way, is built around a single, tubular spar.

The Skipper's engine is the 115-hp version of the four-cylinder Lycoming 0-235, a powerplant that has more than 25 years' of service behind it and therefore, by now, should be about as reliable as a recip can be made.

Beech says that, in designing the Skipper, they emphasized a comfortable, roomy, and quiet cabin. The cabin is 42¾ inches across at shoulder height, which is only one and a-quarter inches narrower than

1979 Beechcraft Skipper 77.

the Sierra. The tinted windows not only provide maximum visibility but the entire cabin is foam-insulated. There is a one-piece bonded door on each side.

The Model 77's landing gear is a low-maintenance spring system that should be practically trouble-free. The nose gear employs an oleo strut and is steerable.

Fuel management is simple for a student learning to fly. There is no tank selector valve, just an ON-OFF selector. The wing tanks feed simultaneously, and in the cabin you have a low-fuel warning light.

Since the Model 77 was still undergoing flight certification tests when this was written, Beech had released no specification or perfor-

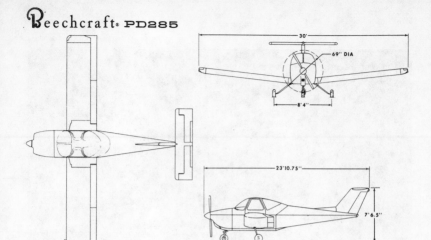

mance figures except to say that gross weight of the production prototypes was 1,650 lbs and wing span 30 ft. And, of course, none will be available to aviation writers until after certification.

It is reasonable to assume, however, that general specs and performance numbers will be close to those of Piper's Tomahawk, because the two are not only almost identical in appearance, but weigh the same and use similar engines (the Tomahawk's 0-235 is rated at 112-hp). Both have the GAW-1 airfoil, although the Model 77 has a lower aspect ratio; four-ft less span and more chord. So, you can expect the Model 77 to be a docile little dude, but one that spins well, recovers nicely, and is a lot of fun to fly. Its useful load should be somewhere around 500 lbs, and it should cruise at approximately 107 kts at 6,500 ft with 75% power.

It won't be fitted—at least, not soon—with Beech's new single power control that automatically adjusts mixture. Apparently, no other Beechcraft will appear with this new feature for a while. Realizing that we hadn't heard anything about this innovation for several months, we asked a Beech official what its status was. He smiled and replied, "Next question, please." We therefore conclude that Beech's single-lever engine control concept is on a back burner, and at a very low simmer, for now.

With the appearance of the Model 77 Skipper, Beech announced that production of the B-19 Sport would be discontinued, the last B-19 having been built August 31, 1978.

8. Musketeer Sport, Custom, Super, Super R, Sundowner, & Sierra

THE MUSKETEER FUSELAGE was re-designed for the 1970 models, giving it a more rounded shape and adding 4½ inches across the front seats. The windows were also re-shaped. The B-19 Sport retained two on each side. The Custom and Super models each had three, with a fourth as optional on the Super when ordered with an extra bench seat in back making it six-place.

Also new for 1970 was the 200-hp Super R, a Super with retractable gear and with four windows on each side standard. The Super R was powered with the Lycoming IO-360-A2B with fuel injection and fitted with a constant-speed propeller. Its list price was $24,950. Other improvements included a re-designed fiberglass cowling, all-new instrument panel with vertical readout gauges, and larger windshield, the bottom edge of which was moved forward four inches.

Both the 180-hp Custom and 150-hp Sport for 1970 were available with an optional aerobatic kit.

Suggested selling price of the 1970 Musketeer Super with standard avionics was $19,850; the Custom was $18,150, and the Sport $15,450.

The Musketeer line continued essentially unchanged in 1971, but in 1972 the 200-hp Super was discontinued and the three remaining craft at last re-named. The undignified (for a Beechcraft) "Musketeer" was dropped and we were left with the Sport B-19, the 180-hp Sundowner C-23, and the 200-hp Sierra A24-R. The most notable new feature on all three models for '72 was the addition of a left-side cabin door, plus the usual new paint schemes.

The 1973 models of the Sport, Sundowner, and Sierra gained some detail improvements. The instrument panels were lowered an inch and

Beechcraft Sport 150.

a-half to improve visibility over the nose; a new quadrant appeared for engine controls, an improved door-latching system was added, and stabilator tab linkage was changed from a 1.65 ratio to a 1 to 1 ratio to reduce control column forces by approximately 50%. Also, a 24 X 30-inch cargo/passenger door appeared at the left-rear of the cabin on the Sierra.

BEECHCRAFT SPORT 19 PERFORMANCE AND SPECIFICATIONS

Seating Capacity: Two- to Four-Place
Landing Gear: Tricycle, Fixed
Engine: Lycoming O-320-E2C, 150 h.p.
Propeller: Fixed Pitch, 74-in. diam.

Maximum Speed .... 140 mph
Cruising Speeds
  @ 75% power, 7,000 ft. .... 131 mph
  @ 65% power, 10,000 ft. .... 123 mph
  @ 55% power, 10,000 ft. .... 113 mph
Stall Speed: (Power Off, 35° Flaps) .... 56 mph
Range: (Including fuel for warm-up, taxi, climb and 45-minute reserve)
  @ 75% power, 7,000 ft. .... 767 miles
  @ 65% power, 10,000 ft. .... 827 miles
  @ 55% power, 10,000 ft. .... 883 miles

	@ 2,250 lbs.	@ 2,030 lbs.
Rate of Climb	700 fpm	900 fpm
Service Ceiling	11,100 ft.	14,900 ft.

Takeoff Distance (15° Flaps)
Ground Run	885 ft.	685 ft.
Total Over 50 ft. Obstacle	1,320 ft.	1,033 ft.

Landing Distance (35° Flaps)
Ground Run	590 ft.	570 ft.
Total Over 50-ft. Obstacle	1,220 ft.	1,190 ft.

Weights
Gross Weight, Utility Category .... 2,030 lbs.
Gross Weight, Normal Category .... 2,250 lbs.
Empty Weight .... 1,374 lbs.
Useful Load, Normal Category .... 876 lbs.

Baggage Compartment
Volume .... 28.8 cu. ft.
Capacity .... 340 lbs.
Fuel Capacity .... 60 gals.
Oil Capacity .... 8 quarts

BEECHCRAFT SUNDOWNER 23 PERFORMANCE AND SPECIFICATIONS

Seating Capacity: Four-place
Landing Gear: Tricycle, fixed
Engine: Lycoming O-360-A4G, 180 h.p.
  Propeller: Fixed pitch, 76-in. diam.
  Maximum Speed .... 151 mph

Cruising Speeds
  @ 75% power, 7,000 ft. .... 143 mph
  @ 65% power, 10,000 ft. .... 134 mph
  @ 55% power, 10,000 ft. .... 123 mph
  Stall Speed: (Power Off, 35° Flaps) .... 60 mph

Range: (Including fuel for warm-up, taxi, climb and 45-minute reserve)
  @ 75% power, 7,500 ft. .... 685 miles
  @ 65% power, 10,500 ft. .... 780 miles
  @ 55% power, 10,500 ft. .... 860 miles
  Rate of Climb @ Sea Level .... 820 fpm
  Service Ceiling .... 13,650 ft.
  Takeoff Distance (15° Flaps)
    Ground Run .... 950 ft.
    Total Over 50 ft. Obstacle .... 1,380 ft.
  Landing Distance (35° Flaps)
    Ground Run .... 640 ft.
    Total Over 50-ft. Obstacle .... 1,275 ft.

Weights
  Gross Weight, Utility Category .... 2,030 lbs.
  Gross Weight, Normal Category .... 2,450 lbs.

Empty Weight .... 1,416 lbs.
Useful Load, Normal Category .... 1,034 lbs.

Baggage Compartment
  Volume .... 19.5 cu. ft. (plus 3.8 cu. ft. on accessory shelf)
  Capacity .... 270 lbs.

Fuel Capacity .... 60 gals.
Oil Capacity .... 8 quarts

A change shared by all three of these craft in 1974 was raising the window-lines one inch at the tops of the doors to gain additional glass area. Other minor changes were strictly cosmetic.

However, the Sierra was re-certified as the Model B24-R as a result of installation of a new version of its IO-360 engine. The new engine had a counter-weighted crankshaft and was fitted with a new Hartzell propeller. A new oil cooler was mounted on the firewall to escape engine vibration, and a new airscoop provided for it. Additionally, the cargo door was raised to include the rear window. An official Beech announcement dated 5 November, 1973, when the '74 models were introduced, stated: "Planned obsolesence is definitely not a factor with the light aircraft during the next 36 months." Seems an odd statement, since by inference one would take it to mean that planned obsolesence was a factor previously, and perhaps subsequently. In any case,

1979 Beechcraft Sundowner 180.

obsolesence, planned or otherwise, has never been much a factor with Beech airplanes. Even the oldest Bonanza, Debonair, or Musketeer is a modern aircraft.

Clearly, when you have a solid design going for you in the beginning, there really isn't much that can (or should) be done to the airframe itself as the years pass. And not much has been done to the Sundowner and Sierra since the mid-seventies. The 1977 Sierra enjoyed some detail aerodynamic clean-up—such as new fairings to streamline the airflow over the main wheels when retracted, strips to reduce the aileron-gap turbulence, and a more efficient propeller—which resulted in a six-knot speed increase, higher service ceiling, and a little added range. Otherwise, the improvements have been minor and largely cosmetic in nature. As previously mentioned, the B-19 Sport was taken out of production as of September 1st, 1978.

There are a few things that should be said about the Sierra. Beech describes it as four-to-six place. That is, for something over $1,000 extra you can get the extra two seats. But let's face it, there really aren't any honest-to-Pete 200-hp six-placers. Four adults, two children, and no baggage, maybe, but that's merely stretching the definition. You don't get any extra horsepower with the two extra seats. All of the 200-hp retractables are good airplanes—good four-place airplanes. None is a good six-placer.

1979 Beechcraft Sierra 200.

Seating Capacity: Four- to six-place
Landing Gear: Tricycle, fully retractable
Engine: Lycoming IO-360-A1B, 200 hp, fuel injection
Propeller: Constant speed, 78-in. diam.

Maximum Speed .... 170 mph
Cruising Speeds
@ 75% power, 7,000 ft. .... 162 mph
@ 65% power, 10,000 ft. .... 154 mph
@ 55% power, 10,000 ft. .... 140 mph
Stall Speed: (Power Off, 35° Flaps) .... 66 mph
Range: (Including fuel for warm-up, taxi, climb and 45-minute reserve)
@ 75% power, 7,000 ft. .... 657 miles
@ 65% power, 10,000 ft. .... 824 miles
@ 55% power, 10,000 ft. .... 880 miles
Rate of Climb @ Sea Level .... 862 fpm
Service Ceiling .... 14,350 ft.
Takeoff Distance (15° Flaps)
Ground Run .... 1,100 ft.
Total Over 50-ft. Obstacle .... 1,630 ft.
Landing Distance (35° Flaps)
Ground Run .... 760 ft.
Total Over 50-ft. Obstacle .... 1,330 ft.
Weights
Gross Weight, Utility Category .... 2,375 lbs.
Gross Weight, Normal Category .... 2,750 lbs.
Empty Weight .... 1,610 lbs.
Useful Load, Normal Category .... 1,140 lbs.
Baggage Compartment
Volume .... 19.5 cu. ft. (plus 3.8 cu. ft. on accessory shelf)
Capacity .... 270 lbs.
Fuel Capacity .... 60 gals.
Oil Capacity .... 8 quarts

The Sierra is the slowest of all the 200-hp retractables because it trades a little performance for a lot of creature comfort and safety. Additional cabin structural members provide a very crashworthy cabin area, a feature that Beech doesn't advertise. The Sierra is licensed in the utility category at full gross load. Its cabin is roomy in all dimensions, comfortable, and the legendary Beechcraft quality is evident in all appointments. Of course, you expect this in a Beechcraft. Once, when we were asking about Beech's quality control procedures, the reply was, "Mister, we've got inspectors inspecting the inspectors!" You will pay for this quality, about $2,000 more than for the Sierra's closest competitor.

ℬeechcraft® SIERRA 200 MODEL B24R

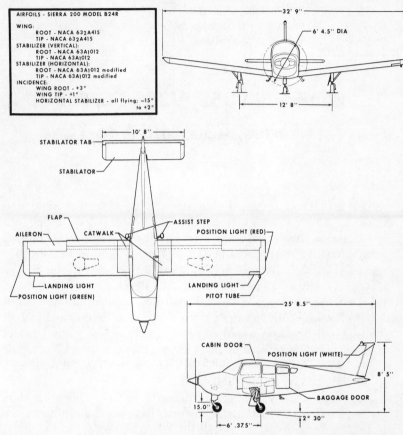

AIRFOILS - SIERRA 200 MODEL B24R

WING:
    ROOT - NACA 632A415
    TIP - NACA 632A415
STABILIZER (VERTICAL):
    ROOT - NACA 63A1012
    TIP - NACA 63A1012
STABILIZER (HORIZONTAL):
    ROOT - NACA 63A1012 modified
    TIP - NACA 63A1012 modified
INCIDENCE:
    WING ROOT - +3°
    WING TIP - +1°
    HORIZONTAL STABILIZER - all flying; −15°
                      to +2°

At the end of the seventies there seems to be little point in listing the base prices of new airplanes, because the actual equipped prices are so much different as a result of the avionics revolution. In 1977 the Sierra's base price was $39,000, although the average equipped (equipped with all those magical black boxes, that is) was somewhere around $60,000. By 1979 the average equipped price was somewhere around $66,000, and it was not impossible to go $10,000 beyond that.

Production of the Sierra, Sundowner, and Musketeer series has averaged about 500 units per year since 1962.

9. Bonanza! V35B, V35B-TC, F33
Series, A36, and A36-TC

THE 1970 Bonanzas gained a few minor improvements in addition to the usual new paint scheme applied every two years. These were quick-opening cowls (screwdriver no longer required), anti-slosh fuel cells, new seats, and improved instrument panel lighting. Performance remained unchanged from that of the 1968–69 models (Chapter 6).

As previously mentioned, when in 1968 Beech decided to re-name the Debonair "Bonanza" (the Debonair had in effect always been a 225-hp Bonanza with an extra tail feather), it was determined that all future V-tail Bonanzas would carry the prefix letter "V" and model changes would be denoted by suffix letters, therefore, the V35A rather than a "W35." And since the 1968–69 V-tails were V35A's, the 1970–71 V-tailed Bonanzas became V35B's.

Entering its 32nd year of production in 1979, this seemingly ageless craft was still the V35B Model. Deliveries had passed the 10,000 mark in 1977.

A number of detail improvements accrued to the V-tails and other Bonanza models during the seventies. In 1972 the cabin was extensively re-worked to give a little more headroom and an overhead ventilation system, while the instrument panel and seats were again re-styled. This is representative of the changes made throughout the seventies. In 1974 all Beech could think of to do to the Bonanzas was re-design the seats again and lower them for still more headroom, while installing a new recessed handle on the glove compartment. The exterior paint schemes continued to change every two years, of course. In 1976 the big news was optional air conditioning.

Beechcraft Bonanza V35B.

In 1977, as Bonanza production (including the A36 and F33 models) approached the 13,000 mark, inertia reels on the shoulder harness became standard equipment; and the 1979 V-tail, along with the other straight-tailed versions, received a 15-degree approach flap-setting allowing extension at speeds up to 175 mph (152 kts). Also standard was a 28-Volt electrical system, previously an option at extra cost, which allows a four-second gear cycle, and additional electrical equipment including propeller de-icing.

Beech returned to single-engine turbocharging with the 1979 A36-TC Model. There are some turbo V-tails around, but the last of those was built in 1970. The first turbo Bonanzas were the V35-TC's of which 79 were built in 1966 and 1967. The V35A-TC followed in 1968–69 (see Chapter 6), and 46 of those were produced. Only seven V35B-TC's were sold in 1970 before the turbo V-tail was discontinued.

The 1979 A36-TC straight-tailed six-place Bonanza has a series of louvers and gills in the cowling to eliminate the need for cowl flaps, a three-bladed propeller, and turbine inlet temperature gauge as standard equipment. The 49 cu/ft oxygen system is standard, a 76 cu/ft system optional. A new extended rear compartment for up to 70 lbs of baggage appears on both the A36 and A36-TC this year.

In 1979 the A36 Model enters its 11th year in the market and now out-sells the classic V-tail. With club seating arrangements and fold-out table, the A36 and A36-TC becomes a flying office or conference room. With all rear seats removed this aircraft becomes a voluminous cargo carrier. The big, double rear doors make this an excellent air taxi or air ambulance machine.

$\mathcal{B}$eechcraft BONANZA V35B

A four to six place, single-engine, high performance business and pleasure monoplane with fully retractable tricycle landing gear. Powered by a 285 hp. fuel injection engine. Licensed in utility category at full gross weight.

PERFORMANCE

HIGH SPEED AT SEA LEVEL
(2,700 rpm, full throttle) ....210 mph

CRUISING SPEEDS
75% power (2,500 rpm)—6,500 feet....203 mph
65% power (2,500 rpm)—10,000 feet...198 mph
45% power (2,100 rpm)—12,000 feet....164 mph

CRUISE RANGE
Range values include 45-min. fuel reserve plus allowance for fuel used during warm-up, taxi, take-off and climb to altitude.
75% power, 6,500 feet, 74 gal. ...... 816 miles
65% power, 10,000 feet, 74 gal. ...... 900 miles
45% power, 12,000 feet, 74 gal. ....1,007 miles

RATE OF CLIMB AT SEA LEVEL
Rated Power, 285 hp ....1,136 fpm
Service Ceiling—3,400 lbs. ....17,500 ft.
Absolute Ceiling—3,400 lbs. ....19,200 ft.

STALL SPEED, IAS (Power off)
Gear down, flaps down 30°............ 63 mph
Gear up, flaps up .... 74 mph

NORMAL TAKE-OFF DISTANCE
(Sea level, zero wind, standard temperature)
Ground roll ....1,115 ft.
Total distance over 50 ft. obstacle........1,870 ft.

NORMAL LANDING DISTANCE (30° Flaps)
(Sea level, zero wind, standard temperature)
Ground roll .... 797 ft.
Total distance over 50 ft. obstacle........1,505 ft.

Performance figures shown are based on maximum gross weights and are the results of flight tests of the Bonanza V35B conducted by the Beech Aircraft Corporation under factory-controlled conditions and will vary with individual aircraft and numerous factors affecting flight performance.

SPECIFICATIONS

WEIGHTS
Maximum Ramp Weight ....3,412 lbs.
Maximum Take-Off Weight ....3,400 lbs.
Maximum Landing Weight ....3,400 lbs.
Empty Weight (Includes Unusable Fuel and Standard Avionics) ....2,031 lbs.
Useful Load (Standard Airplane) ....1,381 lbs.

WING AREA AND LOADINGS
Wing Area ....181.0 sq. ft.
Wing Loading at gross weight....18.8 lbs./sq. ft.
Power Loading at gross weight........11.9 lbs./hp.

DIMENSIONS
Wing Span ....33 ft. 6 in.
Length ....26 ft. 5 in.
Height to top of cabin .... 6 ft. 7 in.

Cabin Length ....8 ft. 1 in.
Cabin Width ....3 ft. 6 in.
Cabin Height ....4 ft. 2 in.
Passenger Door ....36 in. x 37 in.
Baggage Door ....18.5 in. x 22.5 in.

USABLE FUEL
Standard Fuel Tanks (22 gal. ea.)............44 gal.
Optional Fuel Tanks (37 gal. ea.)............74 gal.

OIL CAPACITY
Oil Capacity ....12 qts.

BAGGAGE
Volume ....35 cu. ft.
Utility Shelf ....1.7 cu. ft.
Capacity ....270 lbs.

All Specifications Subject to Change Without Notice

There were two rather confusing Bonanzas built in 1970, the F33 and F33A. The F33 had a conventional tail, of course, but it also was powered with the 225-hp Continental IO-470-K engine. Its performance was the same as that of the E33 produced 1968–69, and discussed in Chapter Six.

The F33A for 1970–71 was built in two versions, the '70 Model was simply a 285-hp straight-tail Bonanza or, to put it another way, it was the same airplane as the F33 but with a bigger engine. In 1971,

1979 Beechcraft Bonanza F33A (foreground) Bonanza A36.

however, the F33A was given the cabin length of the V35B, which meant an additional 19 inches of aft cabin area. It also got V35B max-stability wingtips and other V-tailed options including six-place seating and the large cargo door. The aerobatic version was available only in the "short" cabin configuration, and only in 1970. Just five of these were built as the F33C Model.

In 1972, the Bonanza line contained four models when the G33 appeared fitted with the IO-470-N Continental engine of 260-hp. This is the engine which powered the N35 V-tailed Bonanza in 1961. The G33 enjoyed a rather short production run.

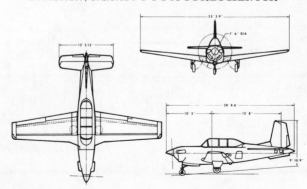

Beechcraft/U.S. NAVY T-34C TURBO MENTOR

Beechcraft/U.S. Navy T34C.

Throughout the seventies production has continued on the F33A and F33C Bonanzas. The F33A remains simply a straight-tailed version of the V35B; and the F33C is the aerobatic version of the F33A. Performance figures for both have remained the same, or very nearly the same, since the conventional-tailed Bonanzas were given the 285-hp engine that powers their V-tailed sister craft.

Now, there is one other single-engine Beechcraft currently in production, a Bonanza spin-off, of course, although it is not available to civilians. It is the turbine-powered T-34C Mentor used by the US Navy as a trainer. It is fully aerobatic and features a fully-reversing propeller for short-field operation. We have no reason to believe that there will ever be a turbine-powered Bonanza; but neither are we sure there won't be. Just in case, we may regard this craft's performance figures as a preview—sort of:

Cruise at 17,500 ft .... 247 mph (215 kts)
Service Ceiling .... More than 30,000 ft
Range at 20,000 ft .... 749 miles (690 nm)
Rate of Climb at 10,000 ft .... 1,275 ft/min
Stall Speed .... 63 mph (55 kts)
Maximum Take-Off Weight (Gross) .... 4,274 lbs
Fuel Capacity .... 125 gals usable
Wing Span .... 33 ft 3⅜ in
Length .... 28 ft 8⁹/₁₆ in
Engine .... Pratt & Whitney PT6A-25 Turbine
rated at 715 shp, downrated to
400 shp
Propeller .... Hartzell three-blade, 90-inch dia